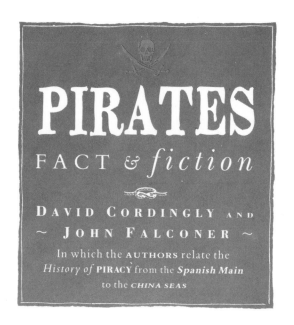

# PIRATES

## FACT & *fiction*

**DAVID CORDINGLY** AND
~ **JOHN FALCONER** ~

In which the **AUTHORS** relate the
*History of* **PIRACY** *from the* **Spanish Main**
to the **CHINA SEAS**

*In an honest service, there is thin commons, low wages,*
*and hard labour. In this, plenty and satiety, pleasure and*
*ease, liberty and power; and who would not balance creditor*
*on this side, when all the hazard that is run for it, at*
*worst, is only a sour look or two at choking. No, a*
*merry life and a short one shall be my motto.*

BARTHOLOMEW ROBERTS

on his reasons for taking to piracy

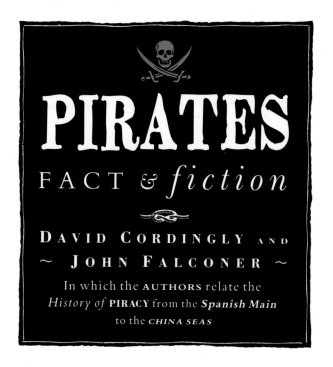

# PIRATES

## FACT & *fiction*

### DAVID CORDINGLY AND
### ~ JOHN FALCONER ~

In which the AUTHORS relate the
*History of* PIRACY *from the* **Spanish Main**
to the CHINA SEAS

## ARTABRAS
A Division of Abbeville Publishing Group

NEW YORK   LONDON   PARIS

Mercury House
195 Knightsbridge
London SW7 1RE

ISBN 0-89660-034-3

First published in the United States of America in 1992 by
CROSS RIVER PRESS
a division of Abbeville Publishing Group
488 Madison Avenue
New York, NY 10022

First published in Great Britain in 1992 by
COLLINS & BROWN LIMITED

Conceived, edited and designed by Collins & Brown Limited

*Editorial Director* : GABRIELLE TOWNSEND

*Editors* : SARAH HOGGETT, JULIET GARDINER

*Picture Research* : JOHN FALCONER

*Art Director* : ROGER BRISTOW

*Designed by* : PETER BRIDGEWATER

## PICTURE CREDITS

Unless otherwise stated illustrations are from the collections of the
National Maritime Museum, Greenwich. The publishers are also
grateful to the following individuals and institutions for permission to
reproduce illustrations:

pp.23, 30 Theatre Museum (Victoria and Albert Museum); p.33
National Portrait Gallery; p.34 (top) Delaware Art Museum; p.35
(bottom) Peter Marsden; p.37 Mander and Mitchenson; p.38 (top)
Institute of Jamaica; p.39 (top) British Library; p.39 Institute of
Jamaica; p.43 Tredegar House, Newport Borough Council; p.49 (top)
National Portrait Gallery; p.53 (left) National Portrait Gallery; p.54
(top right) the Arthur Ransome Collection, Abbot Hall Art Gallery
and Museum, Kendal; p.54 (bottom right) Jonathon Cape Ltd; p.68,
69 British Film Institute; p.74 Delaware Art Museum; p.83 (bottom)
Public Record Office; p.85 India Office Library and Records (British
Library); p.90 (top) private collection; p.90 (bottom) Public Record
Office; p.98 Delaware Art Museum; p. 100 Mander and Mitchenson;
p.113 Brigadier G.H. Cree.

# CONTENTS

Pirates have operated on all the oceans and seas of the world, but there were certain areas which became notorious for piracy and are looked at in detail in this book.

*The Caribbean was the hunting ground for the Elizabethan privateers and the buccaneers of the seventeenth century.*

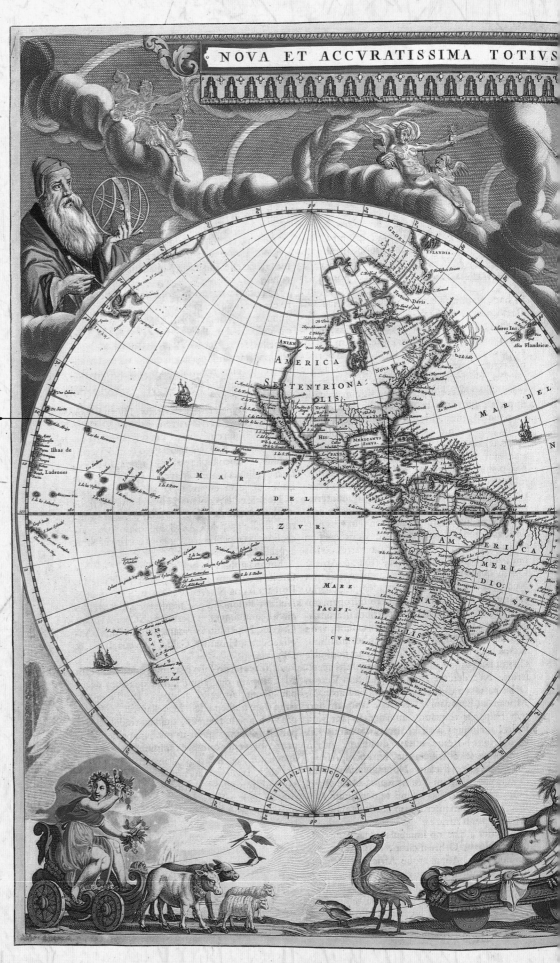

NOVA ET ACCVRATISSIMA TOTIVS

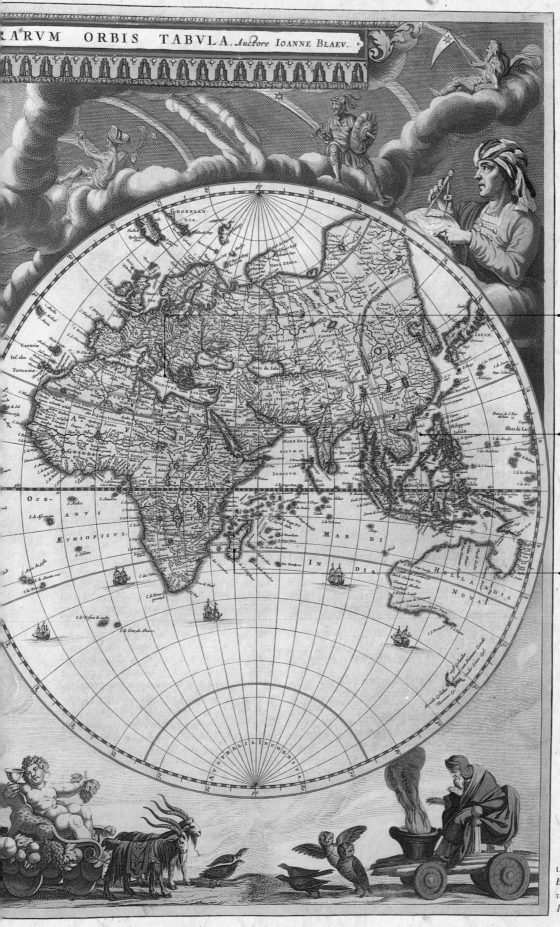

RARVM ORBIS TABVLA. *Auctore* IOANNE BLAEV.

# THE PIRATE SEAS

*The corsairs of the Barbary coast and Malta preyed on merchant shipping in the Mediterranean.*

*Pirates became a major threat to shipping in the China Seas and Southeast Asia in the eighteenth and nineteenth centuries.*

*The island of Madagascar was used by pirates as a base for operations in the Indian Ocean.*

LEFT: *World map from Joan Blaeu's* Atlas Maior *(11 volumes, Amsterdam, 1662-65).*

# PREFACE

This book has been produced to accompany the first major exhibition in Britain devoted to piracy, organized by David Cordingly and John Falconer who wrote most of the text of the book. Pieter van der Merwe has contributed the pieces on Pirates of the Boards and Byron's *Corsair*, Chris Ware the piece on Captain Avery, and Juliet Gardiner the pieces on Women on the High Seas, Pirates of the Silver Screen and the Pirates' Code of Conduct. Leanne Hall carried out background research and compiled the Pirate Miscellany. Lionel Willis prepared the cutaway illustration of a pirate schooner and Peter Bridgewater was responsible for the overall design of the book. The book was edited by Sarah Hoggett and Juliet Gardiner who made valuable suggestions and brought some order to a complex subject.

The organizers have relied heavily on the advice and the writings of authorities on the subject, notably: Peter Earle, an expert on the Barbary corsairs, Sir Henry Morgan and Daniel Defoe; Clinton Black, the Jamaican archivist and historian; Derek Howse, who generously made available his researches on Basil Ringrose; and Charles Reading and Philip Sugg who shared their knowledge and enthusiasm for the theatre and films.

The exhibition has been designed by Steve Simons, David Gosling, John Ashworth and Joy Ashworth of Event Communications, with major input from Rachel Townshend and Louise Ellis. Lighting has been designed by Adam Grater, and the audio-visual installations by Robin Prater.

My colleagues and I would like to thank the Directors and the staff of all those institutions who kindly lent objects from their collections to the exhibition: Margaret Benton, Catharine Haill and Sarah Woodcock of the Theatre Museum; Dr Brian Durrans and the staff of the Museum of Mankind; Dr Helen Forde at the Public Record Office; Vicky Slowe of Abbot Hall Art Gallery; Virginia Murray of John Murray, publishers; David Freeman at Tredegar House; Joe Mitchenson and Richard Mangen of Mander and Mitchenson; and the staff at the Science Museum, the National Portrait Gallery, the Department of Coins and Medals and the Department of Manuscripts at the British Museum, and the British Library. Mrs R. B. Knight kindly gave access to her late husband's collection of pirate artefacts.

We are most grateful to Steven Spielberg and his executive producer Kathy Kennedy for agreeing to the loan of magnificent pirate costumes from the film *Hook*, and for the practical help and assistance of Anthony Powell, the costume designer, as well as Norman Garwood, Gerry Lewis and Jon Anderson.

It was particularly generous of the authorities in Jamaica to lend so many artefacts from Port Royal in the three hundredth anniversary year of the sinking of the pirate city. We would like to thank Sonia Jones (chairman), Beverley Hall-Alleyne (executive director), and Shirley Robertson (curator/administrator) of the Institute of Jamaica; and Ainsley Henriquez (director) and Richard McClure (artefacts officer) of the Jamaican Heritage Trust. We are also grateful to their Excellencies Mrs Ellen Bogle, Jamaican High Commissioner in London, and Mr Derek Milton, the British High Commissioner in Jamaica, for their support for the project. Kate Langley contributed valuable research and, together with Oliver and Jean Cox, made the introductions and paved the way for what we hope will be a long-term dialogue between Jamaica and the National Maritime Museum.

Finally I would like to thank the staff at Greenwich who have, as always, done everything possible to ensure the success of the project, in particular Patrick Roper, Zoë Gamble, David Spence, Gary Stewart, Andy Bodle, Paul Cook (conservation), Barbara O'Connor (loans), Caroline Roberts, Jim Stevenson (photography), Susan Barber, Michael Barrett, Robin Scates, Sylvia Clarke, and Richard Cole and his team.

RICHARD ORMOND
*Director, The National Maritime Museum, Greenwich*

# INTRODUCTION

There is and always has been much confusion between privateering and piracy and this needs some explanation. Similarly the words buccaneer and corsair are much bandied around. All these words have precise meanings. The problem is not the terms themselves but applying the terms appropriately.

The word **pirate** simply means one who robs or plunders on the sea, or as the Admiralty High Court judge, Sir Charles Hedges, described it in 1696, 'Now piracy is only a term for sea-robbery, piracy being a robbery committed within the jurisdiction of the Admiralty'. One of the reasons that pirates were hanged at the low-tide mark at Wapping was to stress the point that their crimes had been committed within the Lord High Admiral's jurisdiction. He was responsible for the punishment of crimes on the high seas and the waterways up to low-tide mark. Above that mark the civil courts took over.

The **privateer** was an armed vessel (or the commander or crew of that vessel) which was authorized by a commission or a letter of marque from the government to capture the merchant vessels of a hostile nation. In the fifteenth century the 'letters of marque and reprisal', as they were called, were issued by the sovereign; but after 1702 they were issued by the Lord High Admiral, and later by the governors of colonies. A letter of marque was recognized by international law and an authorized privateer could not, in theory, be charged with piracy. Maritime nations made frequent use of privateers in times of war because they were a cheap way of attacking enemy shipping and saved the cost of building and maintaining a large standing navy. Needless to say the system was wide open to abuse.

ABOVE: *A swashbuckling image of the Welsh pirate Howell Davis, who preyed on the ships and trading forts on the Guinea coast of Africa in 1719.*

The **corsair** was the term used for the privateers and pirates who operated in the Mediterranean. The most famous corsairs were those of the Barbary Coast of North Africa who were authorized by their governments to attack the shipping of Christian countries. Less well known are the Maltese corsairs who were granted licences to attack the Turks by those martial Christians, the Knights of St John. But just as the Spanish regarded the British privateers like Drake and Hawkins as pirates, so the English, and other Christian nations, regarded the Barbary corsairs as pirates.

The term **buccaneer** was originally applied to the hunters of cattle and pigs who lived on the island of Hispaniola (now Dominica and Haiti). The word was taken from the French *boucan*, a barbecue, because the hunters barbecued their meat on grills in the fashion of the Arawak Indians. Driven out by the Spanish, the hunters joined the groups of runaway slaves, deserters and others who preyed on Spanish ships. By the end of the seventeenth century the word buccaneer was being applied generally to most of the privateers and pirates who operated from bases in the West Indies.

## THE PIRATE OF FICTION

In 1837 Charles Ellms of Boston published *The Pirates Own Book* which summed up the view of pirates which was widespread in the seventeenth and early eighteenth centuries:

> IN THE MIND OF THE MARINER, THERE IS A SUPERSTITIOUS HORROR CONNECTED WITH THE NAME OF PIRATE; AND THERE ARE FEW SUBJECTS THAT INTEREST AND EXCITE THE CURIOSITY OF MANKIND MORE THAN THE DESPERATE EXPLOITS, FOUL DOINGS AND DIABOLICAL CAREERS OF THESE MONSTERS IN HUMAN FORM...

Our attitude has changed since then. Pirates are no longer seen as monsters and have acquired a legendary status. Fiction has taken the place of fact. Long John Silver means more to people today than Black Bartholomew. Captain Hook is a more vivid character than Blackbeard who once terrorized the east coast

of America. The pirates and buccaneers played by Erroll Flyn and Douglas Fairbanks Jr. in the swashbuckling films of the thirties and forties have eclipsed the memory of Sir Henry Morgan and the drunken cut-throats who frequented the taverns of Port Royal in the late seventeenth century.

Much of the material for the fictional pirates of the past two hundred years has been drawn from two books which were among the best-sellers of their day. The first was Alexander Exquemelin's *Buccaneers of America* which was first published in England in 1684. The author took part in many of the buccaneer raids which he describes, and although certain stories in the book are suspect, his work is a valuable source of information. The second

ABOVE: *Mary Read, one of the most famous women pirates, reveals her sex to the fellow pirate she has just mortally wounded in a duel.*

and equally popular book was Captain Charles Johnson's *A General History of the Robberies and Murders of the most notorious Pirates* of 1724. Apparently based on interviews with seamen and former pirates, it includes biographies of many of the notorious pirates of the day. The attractive theory put forward several years ago that Daniel Defoe was the author of this classic work has now been seriously challenged by Defoe scholars.

A few years before the publication of the *General History* a play called *The Successful Pirate* was produced at Drury Lane. It was based on the life of Captain Avery, the pirate king of Madagascar. Even then fact and fiction were confused. Far from living in extravagant luxury on a tropical island, in real life Avery was starving in England. It is interesting to note that a contemporary critic was outraged at the author for 'making a tarpaulin and a swabber . . . the Hero of a Tragedy'.

Lord Byron transformed the pirate into a figure of romance in his epic poem 'The Corsair' which describes the tragic life and loves of Conrad,

THAT MAN OF LONELINESS AND MYSTERY,
SCARCE SEEN TO SMILE, AND SELDOM HEARD TO SIGH;
WHOSE NAME APPALS THE FIERCEST OF HIS CREW,

So popular was the poem that 10,000 copies were sold on the day of publication. In due course it inspired an opera by Verdi, an overture by Berlioz, a ballet *Le Corsaire*, and numerous plays and melodramas, and Byron himself acquired some of the romantic attributes of his hero.

As the real pirates vanished from the Caribbean and the Mediterranean the pirates of fiction took over. Byron's poem and Walter Scott's novel *The Pirate* of 1821 were followed by a succession of adventure stories, plays and

ABOVE: *This nineteenth-century French illustration of Henry Morgan sums up the popular image of the dissolute lifestyle of the buccaneers.*

light operas, and then by the pirate films. It is these, rather than historical accounts, which have created the legends of buried treasure, pieces of eight and desert islands. The old sea dog who sat in the corner of the Admiral Benbow in the opening chapter of *Treasure Island* summed up the image of piracy which was to become embodied in R.L. Stevenson's most famous creation, Long John Silver:

HIS STORIES WERE WHAT FRIGHTENED PEOPLE WORST OF ALL. DREADFUL STORIES THEY WERE; ABOUT HANGING AND WALKING THE PLANK, AND STORMS AT SEA, AND THE DRY TORTUGAS, AND WILD DEEDS AND PLACES ON · THE SPANISH MAIN.

There is a fine ring to this. Stevenson had read the standard literature about pirates. He was much travelled and he knew about ships and the sea. Piracy is indeed full of dreadful stories of torture and murder and wild deeds on the Spanish Main. But walking the plank was never a pirate punishment, and while hanging was certainly the usual method of execution for pirates it was generally confined to the ringleaders, and pardons were frequently granted. Treasure maps and buried treasure, which were popularized by Stevenson and are a key element in Arthur Ransome's *Swallows and Amazons* and many other children's stories, scarcely feature in the histories of the pirates. Apart from the curious case of Captain Kidd who buried his treasure on Gardners Island, most pirates seem to have squandered their plunder on gambling, whores and 'prodigious drinking'.

The true-life pirates were not always so glamorous as the figures created by the men of letters. An English seaman met the celebrated pirate John Ward in Tunis in 1808. He described him as

VERY SHORT WITH LITTLE HAIR, AND THAT QUITE WHITE, BALD IN FRONT; SWARTHY FACE AND BEARD. SPEAKS LITTLE, AND ALMOST ALWAYS SWEARING. DRUNK FROM MORN TILL NIGHT. MOST PRODIGAL AND PLUCKY. SLEEPS A GREAT DEAL AND OFTEN ON BOARD WHEN IN PORT.

This book tells two stories: it examines some of the myths and tries to see how the popular image of the pirate compares with the real thing. Part of the fascination of the subject is

BELOW: *The frontispiece of this early edition of Captain Johnson's classic work on piracy contains a graphic reminder of the perils of the sea-robber's life.*

the number of larger-than-life characters who really existed. Sir Henry Morgan was a commander of genius who carried out the most daring raids with a motley crew in appalling conditions. The exploits of Captain Sharpe, meticulously recorded by Basil Ringrose who accompanied him round the coasts of South America, are as thrilling as any film script. John Ward may have been a short, bald drunkard, but Black Bartholomew, with his crimson damask waistcoat and breeches, feathered hat, and heavy jewellery, was as bold and reckless a pirate captain as the hero of any adventure story.

One problem which faces the writer on piracy is the vastness of the subject. Piracy, like prostitution, has been around for thousands of years. There were Greek and Roman pirates, there were the Danes and the Vikings, the Dutch Sea Beggars and some notorious French pirates. There was piracy on a relatively small scale along the south and east coasts of England in the seventeenth century. There was piracy on a massive scale in the China Seas during the early 1800s when the female pirate chief, Ching Shih, commanded a fleet of 800 large junks and 1000 smaller vessels. This book concentrates on the past five hundred years and takes as its starting point the European discovery of the American Continent.

It was the Spanish conquest of the Aztec empire in Mexico and the Inca civilization in Peru which produced the flood of gold and silver destined for the King of Spain. The treasure ships were the principal targets for privateers and pirates in the sixteenth century, and Spanish merchant ships of all types continued to be the target for the buccaneers in the seventeenth century. From the Caribbean the story moves to the coast of Africa and the Indian Ocean which became the focus for piracy in the eighteenth century. One section is devoted to the Barbary corsairs who roamed

ABOVE: *Dragut Reis, one of the greatest of the corsair warriors, was a lieutenant of Barbarossa and had in his early days been a slave on a Christian galley. He defeated a Spanish fleet near Jerba in 1560, but was killed during the Siege of Malta in 1565.*

the Mediterranean for three centuries, plundering ships and enslaving their passengers and crew. Chinese pirates are not, perhaps, as well known as the pirates of the Caribbean, but they operated on a much larger scale and were every bit as bloodthirsty. These chapters look at piracy as a historical phenomenon, and while it has been largely eliminated along the main sea lanes of world trade, piracy is flourishing in Southeast Asia and in parts of the Caribbean. It may never be possible adequately to police all the oceans of the world, and piracy will survive in one form or another as long as seaborne trade exists.

ABOVE: *Map of the Americas and the Caribbean from Joan Blaeu's* Atlas Maior *(11 volumes, Amsterdam, 1662-65).*

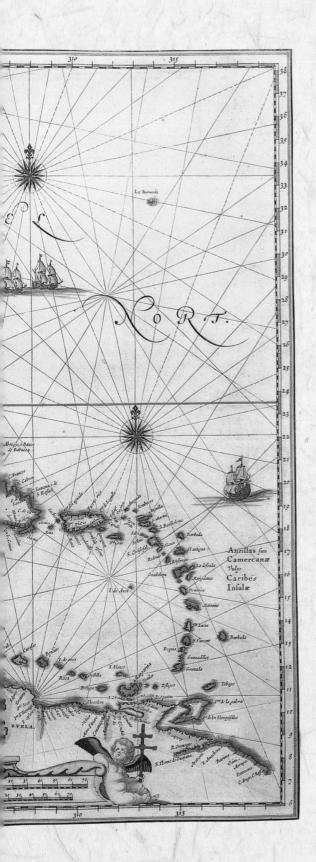

# Treasure House of the World

## THE SPANISH MAIN

'**I** have brought you to the treasure house of the world', Francis Drake told his men as he prepared to attack Nombre de Dios in 1572. The small harbour on the Caribbean coast near Panama was one of the assembly points for the Spanish treasure ships and it was here that the mule trains from Peru and Ecuador trekked with their precious cargo. When Drake and his men ambushed one of these mule trains they found that they had captured no less than 15 tons of gold and 100,000 pesos of silver. It is difficult to assess the value of this in today's terms but it has been calculated that Drake's haul would have been enough to build and equip 30 Elizabethan warships.

Drake was not the first of the sea captains to plunder the treasure house of the world. Fifty years earlier the French corsair, Jean Florin, had intercepted three Spanish ships as they neared the end of their homeward journey from the New World of the Americas. In June 1523 off Cape St Vincent he attacked and boarded the Spanish vessels and found their holds filled with the treasure which Cortes had looted from the Aztecs of Mexico. There were three huge cases of gold ingots, 500 pounds of gold dust, 680 pounds of Aztec

pearls, coffers of emeralds, and other precious stones, Aztec helmets, shields and feathered cloaks, and a miscellaneous collection of exotic animals and birds.

The sheer quantity of treasure shipped across from America was astonishing and it rose steadily during the course of the sixteenth century. In 1516 Charles V, King of Spain and Holy Roman Emperor, received around 35,000 ducats from his overseas possessions. By 1540 this had risen to 165,000 ducats. When the silver mines of South America were brought

ABOVE: *In 1531-33 Francisco Pizarro, with a small force, overthrew the Incas of Peru. Here the subjects of Prince Atahualpa bring the wealth of Peru to Pizarro in ransom for their master.*

into production in the early years of the reign of Philip II, the revenue of the King of Spain was around 2 million ducats a year.

Spain's rivals, particularly France and England, were deeply envious of this new-found wealth. They also resented the Spanish monarchy's claim to colonize and plunder all land in the New World. It was not long before French and English privateers were challeng-ing the might of Spain. At first they attacked the fleets returning laden with treasure. Then they struck at the bases in the Gulf of Mexico from which the treasure ships operated: Nombre de Dios, Cartagena, and Portobello. The privateers were followed by the buc-caneers who usually, but not always, operated with the official approval of the French or English governments. And the buccaneers were followed by the pirates – highwaymen of the sea operating for their own gain. But as far as the Spanish were concerned they were all pirates. When Drake returned from his cir-cumnavigation of the world in the *Golden Hind*, having looted a succession of ships en route, the Spanish Ambassador in London angrily demanded compensation for 'the plunders committed by this vile corsair'.

## OPENING UP
## THE NEW WORLD

Christopher Columbus once wrote, 'Gold con-stitutes treasure and he who possesses it has all he needs in the world', a sentiment shared by generations of European explorers and adventurers who crossed the Atlantic in search of their fortunes.

Unlike the Spanish conquistadors who followed him, Columbus never found gold in any quantity. Indeed it was never one of his major objectives. His constant aim was to find a sea passage to India and the East to open up new trade routes. He failed in this quest but

ABOVE: *Columbus takes leave of Ferdinand and Isabella of Spain as he departs from Palos for the New World in August 1492.*

his four voyages between 1492 and 1504 changed the map of the known world.

The first voyage in the *Santa Maria*, the *Nina*, and the *Pinta* took him from Palos on the south-west corner of Spain to an island in the Bahamas which Columbus named San Salvador, 'Our Saviour', in gratitude for his safe arrival. He stepped ashore on 12 October 1492 after a voyage of seventy days. From the Bahamas he sailed south to Cuba and then east to Hispaniola (now Haiti) before sailing back to Spain to report on his discoveries.

His second voyage took a more southerly route to Dominica and along the chain of West Indian islands to Puerto Rico and Hispaniola where he landed and established a small colony. Columbus vividly described the island which fifty years later was to be the principal base for the buccaneers, and conveys the sense of wonder experienced by the explorers at the strange sights of the New World:

# TOOLS *of* NAVIGATION

The pinpoint accuracy of modern navigational systems makes it difficult for us to appreciate the problems of the early voyagers as they sailed for little-known landfalls, relying on instruments that were often inaccurate and on charts that might give only the haziest indication of their destination. Before the end of the eighteenth century, when precise methods of determining longitude at sea were invented, accurate navigation was perhaps the seafarer's greatest problem – as much for the pirate as for the legitimate trader. For the

pirate did not just cruise the ocean aimlessly waiting to come across his prey by chance: he had to position himself across the known trade routes, which in the days of sail were determined by prevailing winds. And after taking a prize, or when the hunt was up, he had to be able to escape to a bolthole, be it on the massive island of Madagascar, or some tiny Caribbean islet. Just as the seamanship of many pirates was remarkable, so too were their

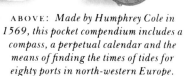

ABOVE: *Made by Humphrey Cole in 1569, this pocket compendium includes a compass, a perpetual calendar and the means of finding the times of tides for eighty ports in north-western Europe.*

LEFT: *The mariner's astrolabe of the type seen here was developed at the beginning of the sixteenth century, and was used for determining latitude. This particular example dates from about 1588.*

navigational skills. The 'pirate round', which took many of them from the Caribbean across the Atlantic to the Guinea coast, and thence round the Cape to Madagascar and the Indian Ocean, required considerable expertise. Like their other stores, standard navigational instruments such as compasses and astrolabes were often acquired by pirates from their victims. A skilled man might also make some of the more simple tools himself: the buccaneer Basil Ringrose records making quadrants (an instrument for measuring the angle of the sun) while cruising in the Pacific in 1680–1.

BELOW: *The octant was used for measuring the altitude of heavenly bodies up to 90°, and was invented by John Hadley in 1731. It was ultimately replaced as the standard navigational instrument for measuring altitudes by the sextant.*

BELOW: *Perhaps the single most important navigational instrument, the compass was in use in rudimentary form in the Mediterranean at least as early as the twelfth century. This Italian example, in an ivory case, was made in about 1580.*

IN IT THERE ARE MANY HARBOURS ON THE COAST OF THE SEAS, AND MANY RIVERS, GOOD AND LARGE. ITS ISLANDS ARE HIGH AND THERE ARE VERY LOFTY MOUNTAINS. ALL ARE MOST BEAUTIFUL, OF A THOUSAND SHAPES. AND ALL ARE ACCESSIBLE AND FILLED WITH TREES OF A THOUSAND KINDS AND TALL, AND THEY SEEM TO TOUCH THE SKY. AND SOME WERE FLOWERING AND SOME BEARING FRUIT. AND THE NIGHTINGALE WAS SINGING, AND OTHER BIRDS OF THOUSAND KINDS. THERE ARE SIX OR EIGHT KINDS OF PALM, WHICH ARE A WONDER TO BEHOLD ON ACCOUNT OF THEIR BEAUTIFUL VARIETY.

From Hispaniola Columbus travelled to Jamaica where he arrived in St Anne's Bay on 5 May 1494. This island was also to become famous as a stronghold for buccaneers and pirates. His third voyage took him along the coast of South America, and on his fourth and final voyage he sighted Honduras and travelled up the Gulf of Darien.

The Spanish authorities were not slow to exploit these discoveries. In 1502 Nicolas de Orlando set up a permanent settlement with 2,500 men on Hispaniola and within a few years had established sugar cane and tobacco plantations. The cattle and pigs they introduced rapidly multiplied and later provided food and a livelihood for the roving bands of buccaneers. Meanwhile on the American mainland near Panama another Spanish colony was established by Balboa.

The expedition that followed was to transform the European vision of the New World. In 1519 Hernan Cortes landed in Mexico with 600 soldiers and 16 horses. The native inhabitants were no match for the invaders, who were tough, professional soldiers, armed with muskets, swords and crossbows. They swept aside all opposition and marched into the Aztec capital of Tenochtitlan. Cortes took the emperor Montezuma hostage and ransacked the great city of its fabulous treasure. During the next three years he effectively destroyed

RIGHT: *Spanish cruelty to the Indians of the New World led to equally savage reprisals. Here Indians pour molten gold into the mouth of a Spaniard, an ironic comment on the newcomers' hunger for wealth.*

the Aztec empire and gave Spain access to a source of unimaginable wealth.

Ten years later an equally astonishing supply of gold and treasure was discovered by Francisco Pizarro in South America. Marching inland from the coast of Ecuador he came across the empire of the Incas. Slaughtering and taking hostages he and his men conquered the ancient civilization and laid claim to the gold of Peru. Within the space of thirty-five years Spain had acquired an empire stretching from Mexico across South America.

## THE SPANISH MAIN

The Spanish empire in the New World was called the Spanish Main. At first this term applied to the mainland but over the years it came to include the West Indian islands and the waters of the Caribbean traversed by the Spanish treasure fleets.

It was these treasure fleets or *flotas* that were the first target of the French and English privateers. Single treasure ships and small squadrons of ships were all too vulnerable to the attacks of swift, armed vessels led by men such as Pierre le Grand and Jean Florin. Dismayed by the losses sustained at sea the Spanish decided to institute a convoy system.

Each year from 1543 onwards two major fleets were despatched to the Spanish Main. One fleet headed for Vera Cruz and loaded up the treasure from Mexico. The other headed for Nombre de Dios and took aboard the gold and silver brought overland from Peru. The two fleets then set off for a rendezvous at Havana on the north coast of Cuba. After taking on water and provisions the combined fleet of around one hundred ships set sail for Spain.

The French privateers retaliated by raiding the ports and harbours on the Spanish Main. François le Clerc was particularly successful at these operations. Known as Pie de Palo, 'Peg-leg', because of his wooden leg he led a squadron of ten warships to the Caribbean and sacked Santiago de Cuba and then prowled along the coast of Cuba and Hispaniola looting small towns as he went.

An even more serious threat to the Spanish colonies was posed by a group of French Huguenots who sailed to North America and established a settlement at Fort Caroline on the coast of Florida. This flagrant attempt to muscle in on her empire provoked the Spanish authorities to despatch one of their most formidable naval commanders, Admiral Pedro Mendez, who set sail from Cadiz with 30 ships and 2,600 men. He captured Fort Caroline in

# BLACKBEARD

Blackbeard is the most famous of all pirates. His ferocious appearance, his hell-raising antics and his violent death have been acted out in countless melodramas, pantomimes, books and films.

His real name was Edward Teach and he was probably born in Bristol around 1680. He served as a seaman on privateers sailing out of Jamaica, but later turned to piracy. His flagship, the *Queen Anne's Revenge*, was a merchant ship of 40 guns which he had captured from the French.

Blackbeard made himself into an awesome figure to keep his own crew cowering in obedience and to terrify the crews of ships he attacked into instant surrender. In addition to his enormous black beard which he plaited and

ABOVE: *The death of Edward Teach, better known as Blackbeard, at the hands of Lieutenant Robert Maynard of the Royal Navy in 1718.*

tied with ribbons, he would go into battle with three pairs of pistols strapped across his chest and slow fuses tucked under his hat. The fuses were short lengths of hemp cord dipped in saltpetre which were lit and belched forth clouds of black smoke.

He did not waste time with captured prisoners. If a victim did not voluntarily offer up a diamond ring, Blackbeard chopped off the finger with the ring which usually caused the other victims to surrender their jewellery instantly. His treatment of his own crew was equally savage. Captain Johnson in his *General history* tells how Blackbeard was drinking in his cabin with Israel Hands, his first mate. Without warning Blackbeard fired his pistols under the table at point-blank range. Hands was wounded in the knee so badly that he was lamed for life. Blackbeard's explanation was that, 'if he did not now and then kill one of them they would forget who he was'.

Blackbeard's performance at sea was less impressive than his appearance and personal behaviour. His reign as a pirate captain lasted less than two years. In 1717 he repulsed an attack from the 30-gun English ship HMS *Scarborough* and forced four vessels in the Bay of Honduras to surrender without a fight. In May 1718 he sailed to Charleston, South Carolina, in company with three other pirate ships. He blockaded the harbour, took hostages, and demanded a ransom which included a chest of medicines. The towns-people gave in, and Blackbeard sailed away after plundering other ships in the vicinity.

In 1718 Alexander Spotswood, Governor of Virginia, announced a reward of £100 for the capture of Blackbeard dead or alive, and commissioned Lieutenant Robert Maynard of HMS *Pearl* to hunt him out. Maynard took two

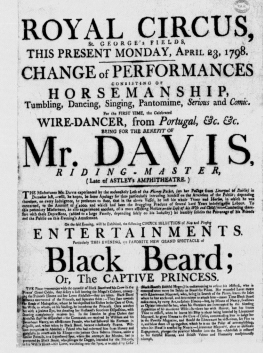

ABOVE: *Blackbeard achieved a posthumous notoriety on the stage. This 1798 playbill advertises a drama in which the pirate kidnaps a Moghul princess who is saved by the hero.*

small vessels and tracked down Blackbeard among the shallows of Ocracoke Inlet. The naval party attacked at dawn, and as Maynard prepared to board Blackbeard's ship, the pirate shouted, 'Damnation seize my soul if I give you quarter or take any from you'.

A confused and bloody action followed in which the heroic Maynard engaged Blackbeard in a hand-to-hand fight on the deck of the pirate ship. Blackbeard received twenty cutlass wounds and five pistol shots before he died in a pool of blood. The battle was to become a pirate legend.

Maynard cut off the head of Blackbeard, hung it from the bowsprit of his vessel and sailed back to the James River to claim his reward. The pirates who survived the battle were tried in Williamsburg and thirteen were duly hanged.

1565 and went on to supervise the fortifying of the key treasure ports: Cartagena, Santo Domingo, Santiago de Cuba and San Juan de Puerto Rico.

It was now the turn of the English.

## ELIZABETHAN SEA DOGS

The first Englishman to challenge the might of Spain in the New World was John Hawkins. Unlike the French privateers who attacked and looted Spanish ships with the blessing of their government, Hawkins was a merchant. His three voyages to the Spanish Main between 1562 and 1569 were first and foremost trading expeditions. They were, however, no ordinary trading expeditions. The first voyage made Hawkins the richest man in Plymouth; the second made him one of the richest men in England. The third voyage culminated in a bitterly fought battle near Vera Cruz in the Gulf of Mexico which revealed the lengths to

which the Spanish authorities would go to maintain their trading monopoly. It also convinced Hawkins and his cousin Francis Drake, who sailed with him on this occasion, that peaceable trade with the Spanish was impossible and the only way that England might get a share of the wealth of the New World was to use force and to plunder.

Hawkins's first voyage in 1562 took him from Plymouth to the African coast of Guinea where he loaded his three ships with 300 negro slaves. Crossing the Atlantic he sold the slaves for a handsome profit to the plantation owners on Hispaniola. The success of the venture secured him backing from the highest quarter for his second voyage. Queen Elizabeth authorized the use of the 700-ton warship *Jesus of Lubeck* as flagship of the squadron, and the Navy Board and City of London merchants were among the investors.

A series of raids on the African coast rounded up 400 slaves but when Hawkins

LEFT: *A portrait by an unknown artist of three of the great English navigators and privateers of the sixteenth century: Thomas Cavendish (1560-1592), Sir Francis Drake (?1540-1596) and Sir John Hawkins (1532-1595).*

# THE SPANISH GALLEON

The Spanish treasure ship or galleon, sailing home to Spain laden with gold and silver from the New World, was the principal target for the pirates operating in the Atlantic and the Caribbean. A typical galleon was a ship of around 500 tons, armed with 60 guns on two decks, and manned by a crew of two hundred men. She was about 125 feet in length, with a beam of 35 feet, and had a notably high and decorative structure at the stern with galleries and a carved lantern. The sealed chests of gold and silver were packed into a treasure room on the lower deck which was boarded up and guarded by soldiers during the homeward journey to Seville.

arrived off South America he found that the Spanish had warned all the trading stations against trading with him. Undaunted, Hawkins went from port to port. By a combination of shows of force with much haggling, he eventually sold his human cargo as well as his cargo of wine, flour, cloth and linen in return for gold, silver, and pearls. He arrived back in England in September 1564 with handsome profits for his investors.

The Spanish ambassador in London was outraged and warned Philip of Spain that Hawkins was planning another voyage. Hawkins assured Queen Elizabeth that his expedition was entirely peaceable:

MY SOVEREIGN GOOD LADY AND MISTRESS, THE VOYAGE I PRETEND IS TO LADE NEGROES IN GUINEA AND SELL THEM IN THE WEST INDIES IN TRUCK OF GOLD, PEARLS AND EMERALDS.

This time his fleet consisted of six ships, with Drake in command of one of the vessels. One disaster followed another. The seafarers had the utmost difficulty in procuring slaves on the African coast and when they arrived in the West Indies they found every port closed against them. Again Hawkins used a combination of force and diplomacy to sell his cargo, but following a storm in the Gulf of Mexico he was driven to seek shelter at San Juan de Ulua, the treasure port of Vera Cruz. He captured the fort overlooking the harbour; the next day the Spanish treasure fleet arrived accompanied by two warships. Hawkins found himself negotiating not with local officials but with the newly appointed Viceroy of New Spain.

In the middle of the negotiations and without warning the Spanish Viceroy ordered his men to attack the British and a full-scale battle

# MAPS *and* POWER

In the days before the widespread availability of accurate printed maps, the laboriously compiled charts of the early mariners were the keys to finding and unlocking the wealth of new territories. And each nation jealously guarded such documents, preferring to see them destroyed rather than fall into the hands of rivals. Inevitably, however, knowledge did spread, and some part in this process was played by the buccaneers, who not only captured such charts from time to time, but in their thirst for new sources of booty pushed forward the frontiers of knowledge and recorded their findings. While the treasure map of literature was a fictional device, the real-life charts of the buccaneers gave access to the true treasure of knowledge and power.

In July 1682 three buccaneers recently arrived from the Caribbean were found not guilty of piracy by a jury in the High Court of Admiralty. To the fury of the Spanish ambassador, who had demanded that the trial take place, Bartholomew Sharp and two of his comrades walked free after a voyage in which Spanish settlements on the Pacific coast of South America had been plundered, causing damage estimated at more than four million pesos, with 25 ships destroyed and over 200 Spaniards killed. Spain was at peace with England when this expedition took place, and this seemed a clear-cut case of piracy. Royal influence played its part in the verdict: Sharp had brought back with him 'a Spanish manuscript of prodigious value' which he presented to King Charles II, which described the whole of the Pacific coastline of South America and gave instructions on how to work a ship into any harbour or port between Acapulco and

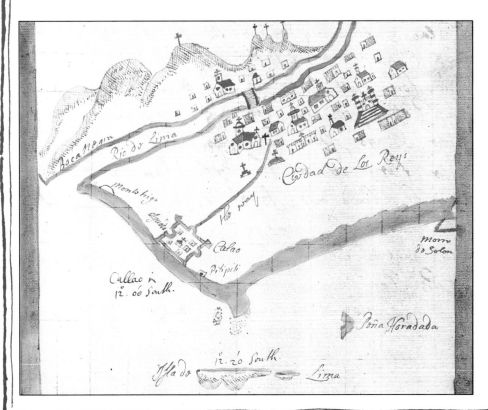

RIGHT: *'The Indians' manner of bloodletting', one of three illustrations of Indian life in Central America in Lionel Wafer's* A new voyage and description of the Isthmus of America *(1699).*

LEFT: *A page from Basil Ringrose's manuscript volume of charts and observations of the Pacific coast of South America, c.1682. This view shows Lima and Callao.*

ABOVE: *The title page (right) and a view of the plantations in the Valley of Paneca (above) from William Hack's* Waggoner of the South Sea *(1684).*

Cape Horn. Sharp had captured this volume from the Spanish ship *Rosario* in July 1681, just before it could be thrown overboard: 'The Spaniards,' he noted in his journal, 'cried when I got the book'.

The waggoner, or atlas of sea charts, was then translated and a number of beautifully coloured manuscript copies were prepared by William Hack. The resulting volume was known as *The Waggoner of the South Sea*.

A fellow buccaneer on Sharp's expedition, Basil Ringrose, also collected information on the voyage, and his journal reproduces a number of coastal profiles made on the voyage, but in addition there survives a manuscript volume of sketch maps and sailing information compiled by Ringrose from his own observation and from the Spanish charts.

broke out. Hawkins and Drake were lucky to get away alive. Drake's homeward journey was uneventful but Hawkins had a nightmare journey and arrived back in Plymouth with only fifteen men still alive. The amount of treasure brought back barely covered the cost of the expedition.

Drake was twenty-nine years old when he returned to England after the battle of San Juan de Ulua. He spent most of the rest of his life waging war on the Spanish. Unlike Hawkins he made no attempt to trade and wasted no time on diplomacy. He specialized in devastating raids on Spanish ships and Spanish sea ports.

Drake's major achievements as a navigator, explorer and fighting sea captain are recounted on page 31. He was without doubt the greatest seaman of his age and after his circumnavigation of the globe was renowned throughout Europe.

But was he a pirate? It is usual to describe Drake as a privateer but the dividing line between privateering and piracy is not easily drawn. Drake was not a pirate in the sense that Bartholomew Roberts and Blackbeard were pirates. They were prepared to attack the ships of any nations indiscriminately, while Drake only plundered Spanish ships. Roberts and Blackbeard hoisted the black pirate flag as they went into action. Drake sailed with the St George's flag of England at his masthead and when he captured a ship he did so in the name of his queen. He told the captain of the *Cacafuego* that he had come 'to rob by command of the Queen of England and carried the arms she had given him and her commission'.

Perhaps the most significant difference between Drake and the pirates of the following century was in the disposal of loot captured in action. Roberts, Blackbeard, and Avery invariably divided the loot among themselves and their crews according to a generally agreed pirate code. Drake took his plunder home and handed it over to the authorities. The treasure plundered from the *Cacafuego* and other ships was taken back to England and locked up in the Tower of London. After a full inventory had been made, Drake was allowed to keep £10,000 and to share a similar sum among his crew. The Queen received around £300,000, and the other shareholders received a return on their investment of £47 for every £1 they had contributed to the venture.

None of this suggests piracy. However, when Drake captured the mule train at Nombre de Dios in 1572, England was not at war with Spain, and when he returned home with his haul in 1573 the Queen and her councillors were so concerned by the effect of his action on relations with Spain that Drake was virtually disowned by his sovereign. He was compelled to go into hiding with his treasure. For nearly two years his whereabouts are unknown and he disappears from history.

It was much the same when Drake returned from his circumnavigation of the world in 1580. He learnt of rumours that the Queen was 'displeased with him, for that by the way of Peru and Spain she had heard of the robberies he had committed'. But the crowds in the streets welcomed Drake as a hero. He was mobbed wherever he went. Ballads and broadsheets celebrated his exploits. Before long the Queen relented and he was summoned to an audience when she questioned him for six hours about his great voyage. To the outrage of Mendoza, the Spanish ambassador, the Queen of England bestowed a knighthood on Drake on the deck of the *Golden Hind* at Deptford amid public rejoicing and lavish ceremony.

The Queen now liked to refer to Drake as her pirate, but his days of unofficial plundering were over. His expedition to the West Indies in 1585 was a full-scale naval operation

# DANIEL DEFOE *and* PIRACY

Daniel Defoe achieved lasting fame with the publication of *Robinson Crusoe* in 1719. The following year he published *Captain Singleton*, a work of fiction which he presented as the autobiography of a real pirate.

Defoe had experienced piracy at first hand when he was captured and briefly held by Algerian corsairs in 1683. It was nearly forty years, however, before he wrote about pirates. He published a factual account of Captain Avery entitled *The King of Pirates* which appears to have been based on interviews which Defoe had with Avery, and these provided him with some of the raw material for *Captain Singleton*.

In 1939 the American academic J.R. Moore announced that Daniel Defoe was the real author of the pirate classic, *The general history of the most notorious pirates*. This was first published in 1724 under the name of Captain Charles Johnson and has influenced all subsequent writers on piracy. Such was Moore's authority as a Defoe scholar that his attribution was accepted for fifty years. In 1988 Moore's theory was demolished by Furbank and Owens in their book *The canonisation of Daniel Defoe*. So convincing are their arguments that there seems no alternative but to restore the *History* to its original author.

ABOVE: *Daniel Defoe, a portrait in the style of Sir Godfrey Kneller.*

THE
# LIFE
AND
STRANGE SURPRIZING
## ADVENTURES
OF
*ROBINSON CRUSOE,*
Of *YORK.* MARINER:

Who lived Eight and Twenty Years,
all alone in an un-inhabited Island on the
Coast of AMERICA, near the Mouth of
the Great River of OROONOQUE;

Having been cast on Shore by Shipwreck, where-
in all the Men perished but himself.

WITH

An Account how he was at last as strangely deliver'd by PYRATES.

*Written by Himself.*

LONDON:
Printed for W. TAYLOR at the *Ship* in *Pater-Noster-
Row.* MDCCXIX.

LEFT: *The title page and frontispiece of the first edition of Daniel Defoe's* Robinson Crusoe *(1719).*

with the open support and finance of the crown. He led a fleet of 21 warships with 2,300 soldiers on board, and his massive attacks on Santo Domingo and Cartagena were acts of war not piracy.

## THE BUCCANEERS
## OR THE BRETHREN
## OF THE COAST

While Drake was causing terror on the Spanish Main, a new menace to the Spanish overseas empire was developing on the West Indian islands where disaffected groups of men from a variety of nationalities and backgrounds were gathering. Some of them had set up tobacco plantations on the smaller islands of St Kitts and Martinique, but had been driven out by Spanish soldiers who had destroyed their crops and burned down their homes. Some were the victims of the decline in tobacco production caused by the competition from the superior tobacco leaves grown in Virginia and the introduction of sugar cane. The harvesting of cane was gruelling and few white men could cope with such back-breaking work in the tropical heat. Negro slaves were shipped across

BELOW: *Costume designs by George Sheringham for the 1929 production of Gilbert and Sullivan's* The Pirates of Penzance. *One of the pirate band (below left), and the Pirate King (below right).*

# SIR FRANCIS DRAKE

Born near Plymouth in 1540, Drake went to sea at the age of fourteen. By the age of twenty he was in command of one of the ships in John Hawkins's third voyage to the West Indies. In 1572 he led an expedition to the Caribbean, attacked Nombre de Dios, captured a Spanish merchant ship off Cartagena, and robbed a mule train of treasure.

In 1577 Drake sailed for South America with five ships led by the *Pelican*, later renamed the *Golden Hind*. He rounded the Straits of Magellan and sailed up the Pacific coast, plundering as he went. His most spectacular prize was the huge Spanish treasure ship *Cacafuego*, from which he took thirteen chests of silver coins, twenty-six tons of silver ingots, eighty pounds of gold, and numerous boxes of jewels and pearls. He arrived back at Plymouth on 26 September 1580, the second man to sail round the world.

By the time of Drake's next expedition in 1585 England was at war with Spain. He launched massive attacks on San Domingo in Cuba, and on Cartagena on the coast of Central America, and sailed home in triumph.

Two years later Drake destroyed thirty-one ships during an attack on Cadiz harbour, and in 1588 he played a conspicuous role in the defeat of the Spanish Armada. He died off Portobello on 28 January 1596, the victim of dysentery, and was buried at sea.

ABOVE: *Sir Francis Drake (?1540-1596), portrait in the style of Marcus Gheerhaerts.*

BELOW: *Charts by Baptista Boazio illustrating Drake's West Indian voyage of 1585-86: the general chart of the voyage (left), and a map illustrating Drake's attack on Cartagena in 1586 (right).*

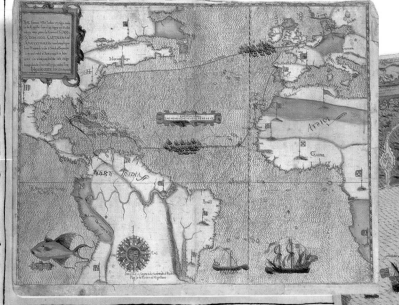

ABOVE: *A buccaneer on Hispaniola,*
*with his hunting dogs and musket, before*
*the islanders were drawn into piracy as a*
*result of Spanish aggression.*

without any habitation or fixed abode, but rendezvousd where the animals were to be found'.

The buccaneers acquired their name from the Arawak Indian word *buccan* (or 'boucan' as the French interpreted it). This was a grill of green wood on which meat was smoked over a low fire. The first buccaneers learnt the technique from the native Arawak people and it became their trade mark.

The typical buccaneer in this early period was a tough and somewhat bloodstained individual dressed in leather hides and armed with an assortment of weapons. He wore rawhide breeches and pigskin boots to protect him from thorns and cacti when hunting in the interior. His shirt was of coarse linen and he had a hat to shield him from the tropical sun. In his belt he had two butcher's knives, and he also carried a sword and a distinctive long-barrelled gun. 'You would say that these are the butcher's vilest servants who have been eight days in the slaughterhouse without washing themselves', wrote Abbé du Tertre.

The buccaneers usually hunted in groups of six or eight. Women were scarce and in this almost exclusively all-male society each buccaneer had his partner: they travelled together, protected each other in combat and when one of them died the other inherited his belongings. It was a companionship like marriage and a close parallel can be found among sailors in the navy who frequently had a mate with whom they shared their life and few possessions. This is a useful corrective to the traditional picture of the buccaneer as a hard-drinking womanizer with a wench in every port.

The Spanish would have been well advised to leave the buccaneers alone to pursue their harmless existence of hunting and trade. But just as they were determined to stamp out the Huguenot settlement in Florida and the tobacco planters on St Kitts, so they refused to

from Africa in increasing numbers to work on the plantations and thousands of white labourers were dismissed.

Many of these dispossessed settlers and redundant labourers headed for Hispaniola where they were joined by a mixed bunch of escaped criminals, runaway slaves, religious refugees and deserters from privateer ships. It was an ideal refuge. The rocky coast provided some protection from Spanish landings, and the huge and mountainous interior allowed a wanted man to lose himself in its inaccessible terrain. The cattle and pigs introduced by the first Spanish colonists had bred unchecked by any natural predators. The early buccaneers roamed the island hunting the animals and selling the cured meat, hides and tallow to the crews of passing privateers. According to the French missionary Abbé du Tertre, 'they were

# WILLIAM DAMPIER

William Dampier (1652–1715) is perhaps the most intriguing figure amongst the adventurers who composed the buccaneer bands: a scientist and observer driven by boundless intellectual curiosity; a man accused of drunkenness, cowardice and dishonesty; a buccaneer; and the commander of an official naval expedition to the Pacific – all these strands went to form his character.

ABOVE: *William Dampier, painted by Thomas Murray in about 1697.*

Dampier was apprenticed to the sea in his youth, and saw varied service before coming to Jamaica in 1674, where he soon became involved with the buccaneers. In the course of his career he travelled three times around the world.

Throughout his travels Dampier recorded his observations, and his accounts of his adventures, *A new voyage round the world* (1697) and *Voyage to New Holland in the year 1699* (1703–9), remain classics of travel and natural history writing. It seems that his years among the buccaneers were no more than a means to acquiring information. In his own words, it was 'knowing that the further we went, the more knowledge and experience I should get, which was the main thing that I regarded'.

---

tolerate the presence of the buccaneers on Hispaniola. In a series of sweeps inland in the 1630s, they pursued the buccaneers and dispersed and destroyed the animals which provided their livelihood.

The buccaneers moved their hunting grounds from inland to the sea coast. They began attacking and looting passing ships and they naturally concentrated on the vessels of the hated Spanish. Around 1630 a number of buccaneers settled on the small, rocky island off the north coast of Hispaniola which had been discovered by Columbus and named Tortuga. It had an excellent harbour and was in striking distance of the Spanish shipping routes through the Windward Passage and along the coast of Cuba. One of the first buccaneer chiefs on Tortuga was Jean le Vasseur, a French Huguenot refugee who had been a military engineer. In 1640 he built a fort on the rocky

mountain above the harbour and armed it with two dozen cannon. Fort de Rocher successfully defended the buccaneer stronghold until 1654 when the Spaniards sent five warships to Tortuga. A force of several hundred soldiers launched an attack on the fort and captured it.

## THE BUCCANEERS IN JAMAICA

By the middle of the seventeenth century, however, many of the buccaneers had moved on to Port Royal on the south coast of Jamaica. This beautiful island of sandy bays and wooded hills rising up to the Blue Mountains had been captured by the British in 1655. They had driven out the Spanish garrison and built a fort at Port Royal to protect the harbour entrance.

Over the course of the next thirty years the English governors of Jamaica encouraged the

# PIRATE TREASURE

ABOVE: 'So the treasure was divided'. *The American illustrator Howard Pyle depicts the buccaneers sharing out their plunder.* LEFT: *Elizabethan money chest, reputed to have belonged to Sir Francis Drake.*

There can be no doubt that what attracted most men to piracy was the lure of treasure. The rewards of piracy could be fantastic and some pirates acquired enormous wealth. Captain John Ward, who made the Mediterranean his hunting ground, captured two Venetian merchant ships in 1607. From the *Rubi* he took 3,000 pieces of gold and a cargo of spices, and from the 600-ton *Soderino* he plundered indigo, silk, cinnamon and cotton worth £100,000.

With the proceeds of these and similar prizes Ward was able to live in splendour in Tunis like an oriental prince.

Even greater rewards lay out on the Spanish Main. It has been calculated that when the Spanish treasure fleet made its annual visit to Portobello to load up the treasure from Peru, there was likely to be 25 million pesos in silver bars and silver coins in the town. This was twice the total revenue of the King of England.

It was part of the pirates' code that plunder must be shared out equally, but even with large crews it was possible for each pirate to acquire a fortune. In the 1690s the Indian Ocean was the richest hunting ground: Avery's haul from the *Gang-i-Sawai* in 1695 is legendary, but his brother-in-arms Thomas Tew was equally successful for a short time, and in 1693 took a ship returning to Bombay which yielded £3,000 per man.

The popular view of pirate treasure is a chest of gold and silver, emeralds and pearls, and pieces of eight. This was indeed the characteristic plunder from a Spanish treasure ship, but a captured merchant ship might also have other cargo which was almost as valuable. When Captain Sharp took the *Santo Rosario* off San Francisco the loot included quantities of fine linen,

and 620 jars of wine and brandy as well as silver plate. In his *True Travels, Adventures and Observations* (1630) Captain John Smith recorded the capture of a Venetian vessel:

THE SILKS, VELVETS, CLOTH OF GOLD AND TISSUE, PIASTRES, SEQUINS AND SULTANIES, WHICH IS GOLD AND SILVER, THAT THEY UNLOADED IN FOUR-AND-TWENTY HOURS WAS WONDERFUL.

Even everyday items were in demand by pirates who could not put into port for regular provisioning. A trial in the Bahamas in 1718 records the theft of £900 worth of 'cargoes, tackle and apparel and furniture' from a merchant vessel. In 1724 John Gow captured a ship returning from Newfoundland 'laden with fish which was of no great value to them'; however, he contented himself with taking 'anchors, cables, sails and what else they found fit for their purpose' before sinking the vessel. And a more basic treasure still is recorded in Edward England's plunder of the East Indiaman *Cassandra* in 1720. As well as £75,000 worth of goods, a surgeon's chest was taken, and 'no part of the cargo was so much valued by the robbers ... for they were all poxed to a great degree'.

ABOVE LEFT: *'Buried treasure', by Howard Pyle. Captain Kidd stands over the treasure that he buried at Gardiners Island near New York on the return from his voyage to the Indian Ocean.*
BELOW: *Pieces of eight, with Spanish and Dutch ducatoons.*

buccaneers to base their ships and crews at Port Royal. They believed correctly that their presence would protect the island from the return of the Spanish and would also discourage the French from attempting to seize the colony.

Port Royal was a paradise for the buccaneers. It was strategically well placed for attacks on Spanish ships heading for the Windward Passage. It provided facilities for repairing and provisioning their ships, and it offered a market for their plunder. Above all it provided them with immunity from prosecution because several governors of Jamaica, notably D'Oyley and Sir Thomas Modyford, were prepared to hand out commissions or letters of marque which authorized buccaneer captains to attack and capture Spanish ships. Governor D'Oyley even organized prize courts for the sale and disposal of captured ships and their cargoes.

When open hostilities broke out between England and Spain, Jamaica became the base for major operations against the Spanish. In 1662 Captain Christopher Mings led a fleet of eleven ships to Cuba and raided Santiago. He took seven ships as prizes and looted the town of chests of silver and barrels of wine. Encouraged by this success the Council of Jamaica authorized Mings to plan a second venture. Later the same year he sailed for the mainland with 12 ships and sacked the town of Campeche on the Yucatan peninsula. He returned to Jamaica with treasure valued at 150,000 pieces of eight.

Mings specialized in commando-style raids which involved landing troops some distance from his target, marching across country, and making a surprise attack on the town from its unprepared landward side. A buccaneer leader who accompanied Mings on several raids, including the attack on Santiago, noted the success of this strategy and used it with even more spectacular results. This was Henry Morgan, an ambitious and ruthless privateer who led a

charmed life ( see pages 42-3). He escaped death on numerous occasions and ended his days peacefully on his estate in Jamaica with a knighthood.

By Morgan's day the buccaneers had become a formidable force in the Caribbean. They had acquired the name 'Brethren of the Coast' and would frequently band together to form raiding parties. It is not known how many buccaneers there were at any one time. The Jamaican historian Clinton Black has estimated that between 1668 and 1671 some 2,600 slaves

BELOW: *Sir Christopher Mings (1625-1666), portrait by Sir Peter Lely. Mings made a fortune attacking Spanish settlements in the Caribbean in the 1650s and 1660s.*

# PETER PAN *and* CAPTAIN HOOK

ABOVE: *The fight on the pirate ship in J.M. Barrie's play* Peter Pan. *This is a photograph of the 1907 production at the Duke of York's Theatre, with Pauline Chase as Peter Pan and Gerald du Maurier as Captain Hook.*

The first performance of *Peter Pan* took place at the Duke of York's Theatre in London on 27 December 1904, with costumes by William Nicholson and some sets by Edwin Lutyens. George Kirby's Flying Ballet Company devised the stage machinery which enabled the Darling children to fly around their nursery before setting off to Never-Never Land with Peter Pan.

The villain of the story is Captain James Hook, the pirate. He is described as Blackbeard's bosun and 'the worst of them all'. His ship is moored in Kidd's Creek, and his crew includes the Irish bosun Smee, Gentleman Starkey, Skylights, 'and many another ruffian long known on the Spanish Main'.

Hook, a caricature of a seventeenth-century pirate, has an iron hook in place of his hand which has been cut off by Peter Pan and thrown to the crocodile. He kidnaps Wendy and the Lost Boys, takes them back to his ship and is preparing to make them walk the plank when Peter Pan comes to the rescue. There is a spectacular fight on the deck, and Hook jumps overboard into the jaws of the waiting crocodile.

The play was an immediate success and has continued to delight audiences of children and adults ever since. Gerald du Maurier played Hook in the first production; Charles Laughton, Boris Karloff, Alastair Sim and Donald Sinden are among the distinguished names who followed him. Walt Disney made a memorable cartoon version of *Peter Pan*, and Steven Spielberg has taken the story into the future with his sequel *Hook*, starring Dustin Hoffman and Robin Williams.

# That Wicked *and* Rebellious Place, PORT ROYAL

On the southern side of the island of Jamaica is a narrow spit of land which snakes out into the blue waters of the Caribbean and provides some protection for the shipping in Kingston Harbour. At the end of the spit is what remains of the once notorious town of Port Royal. Today it is a straggling fishing village, but for a brief period of twenty years, before a devastating earthquake in 1692, it was a thriving seaport of some 6,500 inhabitants.

In its heyday the wharves were lined with merchant ships and the storehouses filled with spices, tobacco, sugar, beef, and barrels of wine. The residents of the town included 4 goldsmiths, 10 tailors, 13 doctors, 25 carpenters, and 125 merchants. There were no less than 44 tavern keepers which helps to explain the hell-raising reputation the town acquired,

and 'a crew of vile strumpets and common prostitutes'. There were also buccaneers and pirates.

Gallows Point, a low promontory to the east of the town, was the scene of numerous pirate executions between 1680 and 1830. The most famous of the pirates to be hanged there was Calico Jack Rackham, who was captured off Negril Bay at the western end of the island in 1720. Two years later 41 pirates from one captured ship were hanged at Gallows Point. Business must have continued to be brisk because in 1725 John Eles, a Port Royal carpenter, sent the council a bill for £25 for the construction of five scaffolds.

Port Royal was also the centre for a form of legalized piracy carried on by the buccaneers and privateers. Originally based in nearby Tortuga, the buccaneers were encouraged to

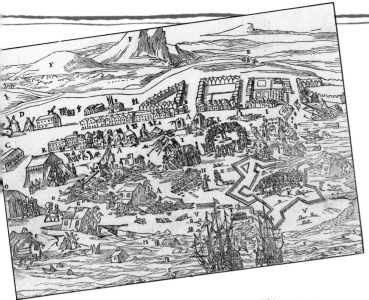

Two thousand people were killed by the earthquake and its immediate aftermath and a further two thousand died later of disease and fever. Two-thirds of the town disappeared beneath the sea. Although Port Royal was eventually rebuilt on a smaller scale and became an important naval base it never recovered as a trading port. The general opinion was that the earthquake was the judgement of God on 'that wicked and rebellious place, Port Royal'.

BELOW LEFT: *Shipping off Port Royal, Jamaica, c. 1760, by Richard Paton. At this date Port Royal was no more than a naval base for the British. The town lies at the end of the spit of land in the middle distance.*

ABOVE: *This contemporary woodcut shows the scene at Port Royal during the earthquake of 7 June 1692. Many of the buildings have been reduced to rubble and several streets in the foreground have sunk beneath the sea.*

LEFT: *These brass buckles and pewter spoons and the stoneware jug on the opposite page are just a few of the hundreds of artefacts buried by the earthquake at Port Royal and subsequently recovered by archaeologists.*

make Port Royal their base by successive governors of Jamaica who believed that their presence would dissuade the Spanish from attempting to recapture the island. The buccaneers were given letters of marque which authorized them to attack Spanish ships. The most successful of the buccaneers was Henry Morgan who ended a career marked by a series of spectacular pillaging expeditions with a knighthood and the post of Lieutenant Governor of Jamaica. It was this town of buccaneers, merchants and whores that was hit by a disaster as catastrophic in its outcome as the volcano which buried Pompeii.

At twenty minutes to twelve on the morning of 7 June 1692, the first tremor of a massive earthquake shook the town. Brick and stone buildings collapsed and along the northern edge of the town the warehouses and two entire streets slid beneath the sea. People trapped by fallen timbers or half buried in the sand were then faced with certain death as a tidal wave swept across the town.

ABOVE: *A romanticized view of a
buccaneer from a mid-nineteenth century
French work, P. Christian's* Histoire
des Pirates *(1850).*

Alexander Exquemelin, who sailed with the buccaneers for many years, wrote a detailed and bloodthirsty account of their methods which became a best-seller and was translated into several European languages. Some doubts have been cast on the accuracy of his stories but there is sufficient evidence from other writers to confirm the cruelty and sadism of many of the buccaneer captains. 'It is a common thing among the privateers to cut a man in pieces, or tie a cord around his head and twist it with a stick until his eyes pop out', one observer noted.

Rock Brasiliano, a Dutchman, roasted several Spaniards alive because they would not show him where they kept their pigs. Francis L'Ollonais, who came from Brittany and settled on Tortuga, was a particularly unpleasant character. On one occasion he made an example of a Spanish prisoner by cutting out his heart with a cutlass, and then stuffing it into the mouth of another prisoner. Even more nauseating was the torture devised by Montbars of Languedoc: he would cut open the

and labourers ran away from the sugar plantations on the island and joined the buccaneers. When Henry Morgan put out a call to the Brethren of the Coast to assemble at Cape Tiburon, Hispaniola, to join the expedition which was to culminate in the sack of Panama City, 33 ships and 1,800 men came to the rendezvous.

The buccaneers employed a variety of tactics to acquire their loot. Their usual method was to cruise off the coast of the West Indian islands in small vessels and to pounce on the Spanish treasure ships as they made their way homewards from Vera Cruz and Nombre de Dios. In swift, lightly armed pinnaces they would sweep up astern of the lumbering galleons, scramble aboard, and terrify the crew into submission by the speed and ferocity of their attack.

ABOVE: *Sir Chaloner Ogle (?1681-
1750), knighted for the killing of
Bartholomew Roberts (probably the most
successful pirate ever) and the capture of
his crew off the Guinea coast in 1722.*

stomach of his victim, extract one end of his guts, nail it to a post and then force the wretched man to dance to his death by pressing a burning log against his backside.

These and numerous other acts of violence and cruelty committed by the buccaneers do not make pleasant reading. They should, however, be set in the context of their time. In seventeenth-century England executions were public spectacles and huge crowds would

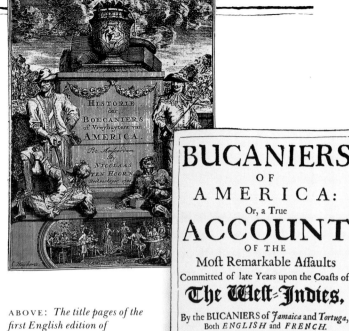

ABOVE: *The title pages of the first English edition of Exquemelin's classic history of the buccaneers of 1684-85, and a Dutch edition of 1700. At least eleven editions appeared between 1678 and 1700.*

ABOVE: *The sack of Puerto Principe, Cuba, by buccaneers under Henry Morgan in 1668. The Spanish put up a strong resistance and only yielded when Morgan threatened to burn the city and kill all the inhabitants.*

gather at Tyburn or Tower Hill to see men hanged, drawn and quartered. The rack was still used in the Tower of London to extract confessions from political prisoners. The cruelty of some planters towards the black

slaves working on their estates in the West Indies is one of the nastiest episodes in British colonial history.

But the voyages of buccaneers such as William Dampier, Captain Sharp and Basil Ringrose do much to redress the balance. Although driven by the search for plunder these men also proved themselves to be fine navigators and intrepid explorers. Their voyages produced a remarkable legacy of logbooks, published accounts, and charts of previously unknown coasts which were to inform and inspire later generations of seamen. Indeed, 'the unparalleled courage of the buccaneers' and the 'greatness of the attempts here related' were for the publisher of Exquemelin's *Buccaneers of America* a glowing testimony to 'the glory of grandeur of valour which here is seen to be inherent to our English nation, and as pregnant of great actions in the present as in the former ages'.

# SIR HENRY MORGAN

Henry Morgan has traditionally been regarded as the greatest of the buccaneers. He launched unprovoked attacks on Spanish colonial cities, and his men used savage tortures to extract information about hidden treasure. But his brilliantly executed raids were carried out with the full approval of the Council of Jamaica, and he had written authority from the governor of Jamaica 'to draw together the English privateers and take prisoners of the Spanish nation'. As a privateer Morgan was acting legally on behalf of the English government as long as he restricted his attacks to Spanish ships. He was not licensed to loot Spanish towns, but his raids were so lucrative that this was overlooked by the authorities.

He rapidly emerged as the leader of the motley crew of privateers and buccaneers who became known as the 'Brethren of the Coast'.

In March 1668 Morgan sacked the city of Puerto Principe in Cuba and followed this with an even more spectacular raid on Portobello. With 500 men he landed three miles from the town, marched across country and attacked just before dawn on 11 July 1668. He took the castle, ransacked the town and negotiated a ransom of 100,000 pesos in bars of silver and gold coins. He and his men were welcomed as heroes on their return to Jamaica.

BELOW: *This recreation of Henry Morgan's battle for Panama in January 1671 shows buccaneers repulsing a Spanish cavalry charge in the right foreground, while stampeding cattle are sent amongst the buccaneers in the centre of the print.*

RIGHT: *An engraving of Morgan from Captain Johnson's history.*

ABOVE: *Portrait of Sir Henry Morgan as a young man, by an unknown artist.*

The following year Morgan led a fleet of ships to Maracaibo in the Gulf of Mexico, but was trapped inside the lagoon by three Spanish warships. By a masterly series of deceptions he fooled the Spanish commanders, burnt the flagship, and escaped under the guns of the fort during the night.

The famous attack on Panama was in retaliation for several Spanish raids on Jamaica, and again had the support of the governor, Thomas Modyford. Morgan and his fleet set sail in December 1670, captured the castle of San Lorenzo on the coast, took canoes up the river Chagres and then made a gruelling march through the jungle to Panama. In the pitched battle fought outside the city, Morgan's war-hardened men defeated the local troops and entered the city.

Morgan's exploits so impressed Charles II that he was knighted and returned to Jamaica as Deputy Governor. There he ended his days peacefully. He died in 1688 of dropsy brought on by his being 'much given to drinking and sitting up late'.

# WOMEN *on the* HIGH SEAS

The tradition of adventurous women dressing up as men and running away to sea, to seek their fortunes, to follow their lovers, or to escape from brutal husbands, is an age-old one celebrated in ballad and song.

There was the fearsome and ruthless Ann Mills and there was Grace O'Malley (known as Graine Mhaol 'Grace of the cropped hair'), the daughter of a famous Irish family of sea rovers whom Sir Philip Sidney described as 'a most famous feminine sea captain' and who fought all her life for Irish freedom from England. But as Captain Charles Johnson wrote in his *A General History . . . of the Most Notorious Pirates* published in 1724, there were two cross-dressing seafarers whose story was so dramatic that it might be thought that it was 'no better than a novel or romance': Mary Read and Anne Bonny.

Mary Read was born at Plymouth around 1690. From birth her mother had 'bred her daughter dressed as a boy', in order to claim an inheritance, and at thirteen, Mary went into service, not as a chambermaid, but as a footboy. But 'here she did not live long, for growing bold and strong, and having also a roving mind, she entered herself on board a man-of-war'. Leaving the sea, Mary then joined a foot regiment in Flanders where she 'behaved herself with a great deal of bravery', until she fell in love with an officer and 'she found a way of letting him [the young officer] discover her sex . . . He was much surprised at what he found out, and not a little pleased'. The young couple married but their happiness was shortlived. Mary's husband died, and 'having little or no trade was forced to give up

LEFT and FAR RIGHT: *The female pirates Mary Read and Anne Bonny, from an illustration in the 1725 Dutch edition of Captain Charles Johnson's* General history of *the pirates.*

ABOVE RIGHT: *Alwinda, one of the earliest recorded women who embraced the pirate life dressed as a man. Alwinda is reputed to have terrorized the Baltic in the Middle Ages.*

In 1720 a British naval vessel captured their ship off Jamaica and the crew was bought to trial. Calico Jack and his men were hanged, but the pregnancies of Mary and Anne saved them from the gallows. Mary died of fever in prison in Spanish Town, Jamaica, in 1721, but nothing more is known of Anne.

housekeeping, and her substance being ... quite spent she again assumes a man's apparel' and rejoined the army. But finding no hope of preferment, she deserted from the army and joined a ship bound for the West Indies. On the voyage, the ship was attacked by English pirates, and as Mary was the only English 'man' aboard, they took her along with their marauding band. In 1717, a general amnesty for pirates allowed Mary to retire, but the pull of the sea was too strong and she joined a privateer from New England.

It was at this time that Mary met Anne Bonny, the illegitimate daughter of a lawyer from County Cork, whose father had fled to South Carolina. Anne had married a seaman, whom she abandoned when she met the notorious pirate 'Calico Jack' (Captain John Rackham) on Providence Island, a haven for pirates. The couple embarked on a daring series of raids on Spanish treasure ships off Cuba and Hispaniola, and captured the sloop Mary Read was sailing on.

ABOVE: *Map of Europe and the Mediterranean from Joan Blaeu's Atlas Maior (11 volumes, Amsterdam, 1662-65).*

# Common Rovers upon the Seas

## The Barbary Corsairs

In 1621 Sir Thomas Roe was travelling across the Mediterranean to take up his position as Ambassador to the 'Sublime Porte' at Constantinople. With him he carried a letter from James I to the Sultan of Turkey, requesting the latter to exercise his authority to suppress 'those common rovers upon the seas who are enemies to the laws of nations and spoilers of the just and peaceable merchant by whom amity and friendship is maintained between Kings and Princes'. The 'common rovers' to whom he referred were the Barbary corsairs of

ABOVE: *Redemptionist fathers negotiate
ransoms for captives of the Barbary
corsairs in this decorative 1649 title page.*

northern Mediterranean by the Christians. In addition, much of the eastern Mediterranean was divided between the Muslim Turks of the Ottoman Empire and Christian enclaves. But stalemate did not mean peace, and the religious struggle continued.

Although nominally under the control of the Sultan at Constantinople, real power in the Barbary states lay with the Dey or Bey, who was elected by the military authorities in each state. Founded on aggressive militarism and religious conflict, it was inevitable that the Barbary states should seek to maintain their economic power and independence by attacking the ships and settlements of the Christian enemy. Although the term 'corsair', which is derived from a Latin word for plunder, suggests illegal activity, the corsairs in fact straddle the line between piracy and privateering: their activities became an institutionalized part of the Barbary states, and indeed were essential for their economic survival. Since the war between Islam and Christianity was unending, it was argued, such pillage was not piracy but privateering, a time-honoured, legal and accepted means of waging war.

And accepted it was, by and large. For while the word corsair conjures up an image of Muslim pirates from the Barbary states of North Africa ravaging the Mediterranean trade of the European powers, Christian corsairs used the same justification of war against the 'heathen' to attack the shipping and trade of the Islamic states with equal vigour and enthusiasm. Licences to privateer against Muslim shipping were issued from most of the maritime states and provinces of the Mediterranean, including Spain, Sardinia, Tuscany, Sicily and Monaco, but throughout the period it was Malta that was most heavily involved and economically dependent on the corsair way of life. A significant proportion of the male population of the island was involved in what

North Africa, who plundered the shipping and coastal settlements of the busy Mediterranean sea lanes for three centuries.

The Barbary Coast states – Algiers, Tunis and Tripoli – had fallen under Islamic control in the seventh and eighth centuries when, in the years following the death of the Prophet Muhammad, the Muslim faith had swept across the Middle East, the whole of North Africa and into Spain. By the end of the sixteenth century, after centuries of war between Christians and Muslims, an uneasy stalemate had been reached, with the southern Mediterranean controlled by the Muslims and the

# TREASURE ISLAND

Over the years Robert Louis Stevenson's novel *Treasure Island* has become the most well known and influential of all books on pirates. Since its publication in 1883, there have been numerous stage versions and four films, including the 1920 production in which an actress played the role of Jim Hawkins, and the Walt Disney production of 1950 with Robert Newton and Bobby Driscoll.

The story is centred around a treasure map which Jim Hawkins finds among the belongings of a sea captain who calls at the Admiral Benbow inn. Jim shows the map to Squire Trelawney and Doctor Livesey who decide to go in search of the treasure. They sail from Bristol in the schooner *Hispaniola* under the command of Captain Smollett. During the voyage Jim discovers that the one-legged cook, Long John Silver, and half the crew are pirates who once served under Captain Flint and are plotting to seize Flint's buried plunder. The pirates delay their attack until the *Hispaniola* reaches her destination, but their attempts to recover the treasure are foiled by Ben Gunn, who has his revenge on the pirates who had marooned him on the island three years earlier.

Part of the appeal of the story is that it has such an authentic ring about it, especially the passages on board the schooner. Stevenson was not an experienced seaman but his father was a harbour engineer, and his own travels included an extended trip on the French canals, and a voyage to America. He was familiar with Captain Johnson's *General history of the pirates* and he created a band of wily and murderous ruffians whose behaviour and mannerisms are wholly convincing. However, his most memorable creation, Long John Silver, was not based on a pirate, but on his one-legged friend W.E. Henley, a writer and poet with a flamboyant and powerful personality. Stevenson himself wrote, 'I was not a little proud of John Silver...and to this day rather admire that smooth and formidable adventurer'.

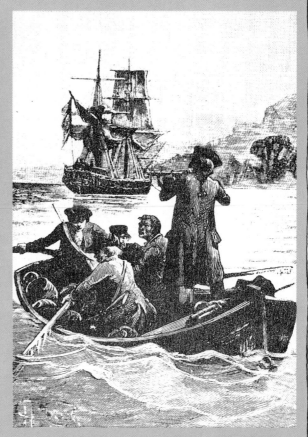

ABOVE: *Squire Trelawney fires at the pirates who have taken command of the* Hispaniola. *From the first illustrated edition of* Treasure Island, *published in 1885.*

TOP: *Robert Louis Stevenson, painted by Sir William Blake Richmond in 1887.*

ABOVE: *Ali Khoja, who became ruler of Algiers after the bombardment of 1816, and was infamous for his fondness for European women in his harem. His rule was cut short by his death from plague in 1818.*

was seen as a perfectly respectable, indeed honourable, profession. Licences issued from the island came with the full authority of the Grand Master of the Knights of St John of Jerusalem, the militant Christian charity which had been installed on the island by the Emperor Charles V in 1530 as a bulwark against the advance of Islam in the Mediterranean.

## THE GALLEYS

One of the significant differences between the corsairs of the Mediterranean and the pirates of other oceans was their favoured booty. The Muslim and Christian corsairs plundered each other's ships, but for both the most sought-after commodity was the human cargo. Slaves were valuable both as manpower and for potential ransom, and over the years a well-administered and extremely profitable system developed by which go-betweens (often members of religious orders) negotiated and administered the release of captives. One reason for the high demand for slaves lay in the type of ship used by both Muslim and Christian corsairs in the Mediterranean, the galley. Mortality was high among the slaves who worked the oars, and the worst fate for a captured prisoner on either side was to be condemned to the galleys as a rower. The design of the galley was well adapted to the enclosed waters of the Mediterranean. A typical Muslim galley was some 180 feet long by about 16 feet wide, and carried one mast for sailing when not in action. The greater part of the length was taken up by the banks of benches where the oarsmen were chained, up

ABOVE: '*Spanish men-of-war engaging Barbary corsairs*',
by Cornelis Vroom, 1615. Spain had been a scene of conflict
between Christians and Muslims for centuries.

to six men to a heavy 15-foot oar; down the centre of the benches ran a gangway from which the overseer would spur on the rowers to even greater exertions – either by shouted encouragement or by liberal use of the whip. The Muslim galleys mounted a large gun in the bows behind the massive ram, and this was fired to clear the enemy's decks as they came alongside. The galleys themselves were not heavily armed, since the invariable tactic of the Muslim corsairs was to ram the enemy and board her. The fighting men would scramble across with muskets and scimitars, overpowering opposition in hand-to-hand combat. The rowers took no part in the fighting itself, since as captured prisoners their sympathies were obviously suspect, and they were chained to

their oars during the battle. Christian slaves were also forbidden from going near either the tiller or the compass of a Muslim galley.

The galley was designed for short cruises, and most voyages probably did not exceed two months. Speed was their most important asset, and a ship required frequent careening in order to scrape off the growth of weeds and to wax the hull so that it would glide through the water. Many of the corsair ships also had safe havens on remote islands or stretches of coastline, where they could lie up during a voyage and take on water and provisions. Miguel de Cervantes in *Don Quixote* also describes the even shorter raids that were standard practice among the corsairs near the Spanish coast. Corsairs from Tetouan in Morocco, for

BELOW: *The layout of a Barbary galley, with its massive ram, bow cannon and single mast, is clearly seen in this seventeenth-century engraving.*

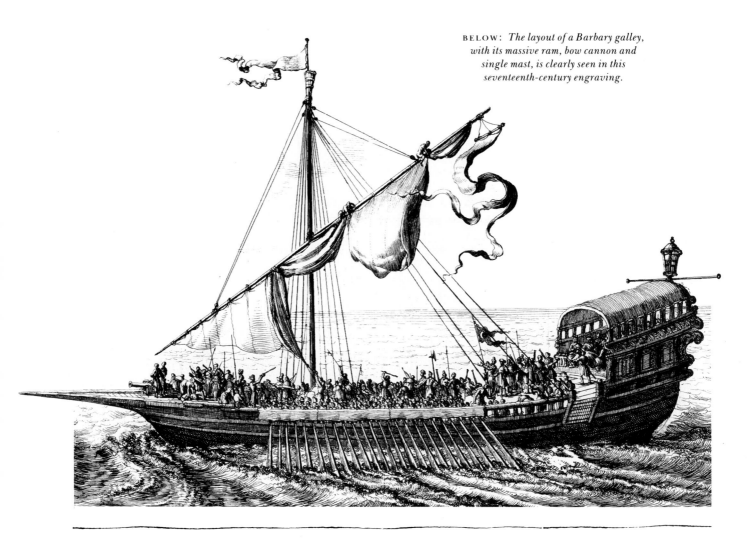

# BYRON'S
# CORSAIR

*T*he *Corsair*, published in 1814, tells the story of Conrad, an Aegean pirate whose sole virtue is his sense of honour.

Lord Byron (1788–1824) was the most heroic and sensational of the English romantic poets. He shot to fame in 1812 with *Childe Harold's Pilgrimage* (Cantos I and II) and such was public fascination with him and his theme of the piratical outcast that *The Corsair* sold a staggering 10,000 copies on its first day of publication. It appeared when the Barbary states were in final decline. As the real threat faded, so the corsair could be romanticized as a heroic but doomed outsider; no longer lethal but still charged with exotic danger.

Byron's poem has inspired at least six operas, including one by Verdi, a well-known ballet (1856) and an overture by Berlioz.

ABOVE: *Lord Byron, painted by Thomas Phillips in 1813.*

example, would set sail at night for Spain in search of prizes, and return home the next day with whatever booty they had seized in the short foray.

In command of the Muslim galley was the *rais* or captain, generally a European renegade or a Turk, and often the owner of the ship as well. Almost as important as the *rais* was the Agha of Janissaries, who commanded the fighting men and who was consulted on all matters relating to the attack. The janissaries themselves, a body of fighting men renowned for their courage and discipline, were generally far better treated than their Christian counterparts, and a Muslim galley might carry as many as 150 of them. A scribe was also taken on each voyage, and it was his task to compile an inventory of goods and prisoners captured. These prizes were later shared out

ABOVE: *The capture of Tunis by the forces of Charles V of Spain in 1535.*

according to a carefully calculated scale. A certain amount of looting of the personal effects of passengers took place immediately after the capture of a ship, but the main cargo was all taken back to port. In the 1630s between ten and twelve per cent was reserved for the Pasha (depending on the state), with a further one per cent port fee. After a few further deductions, the remainder was divided in two parts, one half of which went to the owner or owners, the other half to the ship's company. This crew's half was in turn further sub-divided: the *rais* received between ten and fifteen per cent, the senior officers three per cent, the janissaries two per cent. A small allocation was also made to the slaves who rowed the galleys, but this would be surrendered to their owners, who might make substantial sums by hiring labour for the galleys.

Although the vessels of both Muslim and Christian corsairs conformed to the galley

# SWALLOWS and AMAZONS

In Arthur Ransome's classic adventure stories about children and boats, piracy is a central theme. In *Swallows and Amazons*, which was first published in 1930, Nancy and Peggy Blackett play the part of pirates and fly the Jolly Roger from the mast of their 14-foot dinghy. They have an uncle they call Captain Flint who is a retired pirate and lives on a houseboat with a green parrot. *Peter Duck*, which was published in 1932, takes John, Susan, Titty, Roger, Nancy and Peggy to the Caribbean in search of buried pirate treasure. *Missee Lee* is a story about Chinese pirates. The central character is based on Madame Sun Yat Sen, the Chinese revolutionary leader. The books were particularly popular in the 1930s and 1940s.

ABOVE: *Arthur Ransome, a portrait by Violet Trefusis in 1930.*
RIGHT: *This illustration by Arthur Ransome for* Swallows and Amazons *shows Captain John rowing the* Swallow *past Captain Flint's houseboat.*

ABOVE: *British sailors boarding an Algerine corsair, an early nineteenth-century engraving.*

FAR RIGHT: *Turks attacking a Greek corsair.*

type, there were significant points of differ-ence between the two, both in the ships them-selves and in the crewing arrangements. The Christian vessels were on the whole larger and less manoeuvrable than their Muslim counter-parts, and often had two or even three masts. Sacrificing all for speed in the water, the Muslim galleys carried more oarsmen pro-portional to their length, and did away with all non-functional decorative features apart from flags. Their single bow-chaser cannon con-trasted with the three found on Christian boats, and the gunnery of the Muslim corsairs tended to be of generally poor quality since they relied on close-quarter fighting. The Maltese corsairs, on the other hand, had a high reputation for their gunnery, and relied much

more heavily on artillery. Discipline on board the Christian ships appears to have been far more lax and more democratic than that of the Muslims. And while there were seldom arguments about the division of the spoils amongst the Muslims, disagreements and court cases were commonplace in Malta.

## LIFE IN THE *BAGNIO*

For those unfortunates taken by the corsairs, whether at sea or during one of their frequent coastal raids, a new and harsh world awaited, one which might be theirs for no longer than it took to arrange an agreed ransom, or one in which they might live for the rest of their lives. For those lucky few who could prove that they

THE
CASE
Of many HUNDREDS
OF
Poor English-Captives,
IN
ALGIER,
TOGETHER,
With some Remedies
To Prevent their Increase, Humbly Represented to
Both HOUSES of
PARLIAMENT.

THat there hath been taken, since their last breach with us, not less than an Hundred and Forty Sail of Ships and other Vessels, many of them being richly laden, besides the great Advance they make upon the persons they take, there being at this time upwards of 1500, (besides many Hundreds who have Dyed there of the Plague,) who suffer and undergo most miserable Slavery, put to dayly extream and difficult Labour, but a poor supply of Bread and Water for their Food, stripped of their Cloaths and covering, and their Lodging on the cold Stones and Bricks; but what is more, their extream hard and savage lading them sometimes with great burthens of Chains, and shut up in noisome places, commonly adding some hundreds of blows on their bare feet, forcing out the very Blood, and sometimes on the Back, sometimes on the Belly, and sometimes on them all, insomuch that many are long decripit, some for ever, and some dying under their hands. But above all, is their frequent forcing of Men and Boys by their execrable Sodomy, also their inhumane abuses and force to the Bodies of Women and Girls, frequently attempting Sodomy on them also, some of whom both Males and Females have been so abused as hardly to escape with their Lives; All which Usage is so notoriously known by those who have been redeemed thence, that it needs no proof.

*First,*

ABOVE: *A seventeenth-century broadsheet petitioning Parliament to take action over the 1500 English citizens held in captivity in the Barbary states.*

were citizens of a country who had a treaty with the Barbary state to which they had been taken, freedom might come immediately. The remainder were taken to the *bagnio*, an extensive courtyard complex where the slaves were housed. And here they entered a world within a world, with its own customs, hierarchies, language and punishments. First came the auction, during which the new captives would be humiliatingly paraded before prospective purchasers. If they were bought for a private household, they might, if they were lucky in

## THE BROTHERS BARBAROSSA

HORUSCE en HAREADEN BARBAROSSA

The consolidation of Barbary power in the Mediterranean owed more to two brothers of humble Greek parentage than to any other individuals. Aruj and Khair-ed-Din, known as the Brothers Barbarossa or 'Redbeard', arrived in North Africa in the early years of the sixteenth century. At the start of their careers it seems that Aruj was the dominant brother. Gaining the protection and patronage of the King of Tunis in return for a share of his booty, Aruj set about building up a powerful pirate fleet. In 1504 he captured two treasure galleys flying the flag of Pope Julius II, and in the following years plundered ships and settlements across the Mediterranean. In 1516 he seized Algiers, but was killed two years later when the Spanish sent a force of 10,000 men against him.

His brother Khair-ed-Din was an equally valiant fighter, but possessed qualities of statesmanship as well. After his brother's death, he allied himself to the Ottoman Emperor Sultan Selim I, and in return for his loyalty was appointed Governor-General of Algiers and sent a force of 2,000 janissaries. As Admiral of the Sultan's fleets he raided the coasts of the Christian Mediterranean, and re-took several towns held by the Spanish in North Africa. By the time of his death in 1546 Khair-ed-Din had made the Muslim forces in the Mediterranean both feared and respected.

ABOVE AND FAR LEFT: *Horrific punishments were meted out to Christian captives of the corsairs, although the relish with which these were illustrated in contemporary accounts suggests a propagandist motive.*

their new masters, look forward to a tolerable existence of domestic service. For the *beylik*, or state-owned slave, the outlook was grimmer, and the *bagnio* would become his new home. On arrival each slave would have a heavy iron ring and chain riveted around his ankle, although a well-placed bribe might secure a lighter chain or even none at all. Next the slave would be registered and issued with basic clothing and a blanket. Many now faced a life

ABOVE: *Slaves being landed at Algiers, c.1700.*

of servitude and hard physical toil, employed in such back-breaking tasks as quarrying and shifting rocks for public works. The meagre ration of bread provided was quite insufficient for such hard work, and in some states it was standard practice for the slaves to end their work in the early afternoon so that they might go off in search of food, or practise a craft from the proceeds of which they might buy nourishment. The enclosed world of the *bagnio* was further emphasized by the taverns and shops within its precincts. By bribing the overseers an inmate might be excused manual labour altogether and be permitted to follow a craft in the workshops, and sometimes even in the town outside as long as he returned at night to the *bagnio* (better sleeping quarters

were of course also available at a price). Over the years there evolved the *lingua franca* of the Barbary Coast, a simplified mixture of tongues (mainly Spanish and Italian) by which the slaves of various nations could communicate.

The Spanish author Miguel de Cervantes was captured by corsairs in 1575 and remained a prisoner in Algiers until 1580, despite several daring attempts at escape. Many of his experiences from this time found their way into *Don Quixote* in the story told by the escaped slave. 'Hunger and nakedness' was their lot, but these were minor burdens compared with other punishments that might by handed out, particularly for offences against the Islamic religion or against the person of a Muslim: Cervantes describes hangings, beatings and impalements as everyday occurrences. No doubt Christian propaganda played its part in stressing both the ingenuity and frequency of the cruelties to which the slaves were subjected, but there is sufficient other documentary evidence for us to be certain that such punishments did take place, and often for insignificant offences.

## 'TURNING TURK'

One of the few ways of improving his lot for the slave with little hope of ransom was to 'turn Turk' and renounce his religion. Although

renouncing Christianity did not automatically mean an end to slavery, a convert to Islam could not be fettered and, perhaps most important of all, would not be sent to row in a galley. But such was the constant demand for slaves for the galleys that, ironically in view of Islam's proselytizing nature, strong and healthy men who would make good rowers might well be forcibly prevented from changing their faith.

Embracing Islam was a serious step to take, since for all but a few it effectively severed a man's ties with his former life. Particularly brutal punishments were reserved for those who attempted to revert to Christianity, and they could expect to die at the stake or in even more terrible ways, while renegade corsairs captured by Christian ships could expect little mercy. A common form of insurance for those who had foresworn the Christian religion during their captivity was to collect passes or affidavits from their fellows testifying that in

BELOW: *Slaves attempt to escape from the Barbary coast in an open boat. Only a small number of the corsairs' prisoners succeeded in escaping from captivity.*

their heart of hearts they remained true Christians. Cervantes records this practice, as well as the more opportunistic use to which these passes were sometimes put by renegade corsairs, who carried them in case they were captured by Christian ships. This carried its own risk, since to be caught with them by the Muslims would mean certain death.

## THE RENEGADE CORSAIRS

Possibly the greatest blow dealt to Europe by the converts to Islam was in the transfer of technology and knowledge to the Barbary states at a time when Europe had been rapidly overtaking and outstripping Islam in these fields. For, more than any other single group, it was the seamen who supplied the Barbary states with pilots familiar with European waters outside the Mediterranean, who gave them information on the best places to plunder and the state of their enemies' defences, who cast their guns and trained them in their use. Such was the premium placed on this new knowledge in Barbary that for a time Europeans were accepted as corsairs operating out of the North African ports without formally renouncing the Christian religion. The unruly element they introduced was also ignored for the sake of their knowledge and seafaring skills. Sieur de Breves reported in 1606 on the 'profuse liberality and excessive debauches' of the English corsairs which were permitted at Algiers:

> THEY CARRY THEIR SWORDS AT THEIR SIDES, THEY RUN DRUNK THROUGH THE TOWN ... THEY SLEEP WITH THE WIVES OF THE MOORS ... IN BRIEF, EVERY KIND OF DEBAUCHERY AND UNCHECKED LICENCE IS PERMITTED TO THEM ...

Once the secrets of European maritime technology had been learnt the hard way, however,

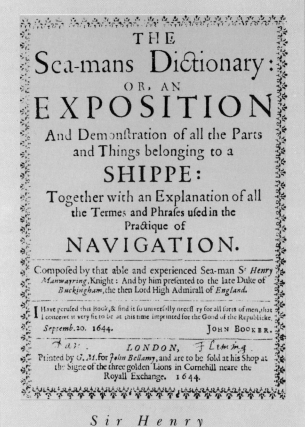

*Sir Henry*

# MAINWARING

Sir Henry Mainwaring experienced piracy from both sides of the law. In 1612 he fitted out the ship *Resistance* and set himself up as a pirate on the Moroccan coast. In a series of successful raids against Spanish shipping he accumulated great wealth, and in 1614 voyaged as far afield as Newfoundland. In 1616 he returned to England to an official pardon and a career of high office.

In 1617, his *Discourse of the beginnings, practices and suppression of pirates* appeared, but perhaps his most important work was *The seaman's dictionary*, the first authoritative English work on seamanship, written in the 1620s, but not published until 1644.

ABOVE: *Title page of Sir Henry Mainwaring's* The seaman's dictionary, *first published in 1644.*

the Muslims became less tolerant of this behaviour.

The sea captains who sought the protection of the Barbary states also brought with them formidable fighting skills which further strengthened the corsair threat to Mediterranean trade. The early years of the seventeenth century produced a particularly rich harvest of such characters. The end of the Spanish War in 1603 found the ports of Europe full of unemployed seamen, many of them ex-privateers who overnight had been transformed from valuable servants of their country to unwanted and often unruly embarrassments. Such a one was John Ward, a fisherman who had joined the English navy and risen through the ranks to command the King's ship *Lion's Whelp*. In the early 1600s he was to be found in the taverns of Portsmouth, inciting his comrades to mutiny and looking back fondly to the old privateering days:

'SBLOOD, WHAT WOULD YOU HAVE ME SAY, WHERE ARE THE DAYS THAT HAVE BEEN, AND THE SEASONS THAT WE HAVE SEEN, WHEN WE MIGHT SING, SWEAR, DRINK, DRAB AND KILL MEN AS FREELY AS YOUR CAKEMAKERS DO FLIES? WHEN WE MIGHT DO WHAT WE LIST, AND THE LAW WOULD BEAR US OUT IN'T, NAY WHEN WE MIGHT LAWFULLY DO THAT, WE SHALL BE HANGED FOR AN WE DO NOW, WHEN THE WHOLE SEA WAS OUR EMPIRE, WHERE WE ROBB'D AT WILL, AND THE WORLD BUT OUR GARDEN WHERE WE WALKED FOR SPORT?

Turning to piracy, Ward placed himself under the protection of the Dey of Tunis. Within a short time he commanded a fleet of ten ships, and was among the most feared corsair captains in the Mediterranean. By 1609 he was the subject of balladeers and pamphleteers in London, who condemned his treachery in allying himself to a Muslim master, while

enviously listing the splendours of his residence, 'a very stately house in Tunis, rich with marble and alabaster, more fit for a prince than a pirate'. He appears to have wearied of this life, however, and sought a pardon, but his approaches met with little response, and he finally burned his bridges, converting to Islam

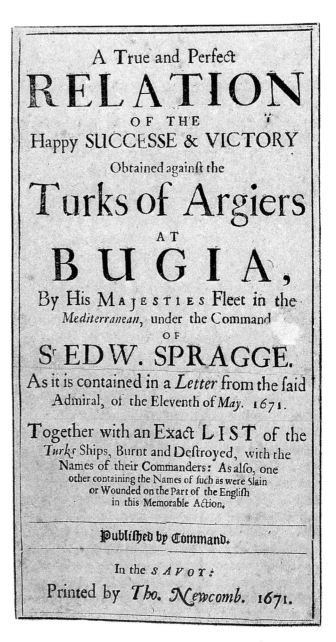

ABOVE: *A pamphlet celebrating Sir Edward Spragge's attack on and destruction of eight Algerine corsairs in Bougie Bay east of Algiers in May 1671.*

ABOVE: *The bombardment of Algiers by an Anglo-Dutch squadron under the command of Lord Exmouth in August 1816 brought about the release of over 3,000 Christian captives from the North African states. But it was not until 1830, with the French occupation of Algiers, that the Barbary threat was finally ended.*

and taking the name Yusuf Rais. He died of the plague in Tunis in about 1622.

*The Ballad of Danseker the Dutchman* records a partnership between Ward and the other most celebrated of the Europeans who joined the ranks of the Barbary corsairs. Simon Danziger (sometimes known as Danser) operated as a corsair out of Marseilles before transferring his base to Algiers. Here his success earned him the nickname *Dali Capitan*, Captain Devil, but he incurred the wrath of his hosts by obstinately refusing to renounce his religion. By 1608 he was attempting to negotiate a return to France, where he had left his family. He manned his ship with sailors of various nationalities, and after taking a valuable prize of a Spanish galleon, he returned to Marseilles. All would have been well had he stayed where he was, but in 1611 he went to Tunis to ransom some captured French vessels, and was arrested and hanged on the orders of the Dey, his previous master.

But Danziger's importance lies not with the value of the prizes he took, for according to Father Dan (who was in Algiers in the 1630s and wrote an important history of the Barbary states) he more than anyone was responsible for introducing the 'round ship' of northern Europe as an alternative to the traditional rowed galley of the Mediterranean. This was to have far-reaching effects, for these ships allowed the corsairs to break out of the Mediterranean and to extend their field of operations to the Atlantic. Their stouter construction and improved sailing qualities enabled the corsairs to brave the heavier seas and greater distances of the Atlantic, and this in turn led to the rise of the Moroccan port of Salé as a base for piracy. From here, encouraged by reports of the weakness of the English navy, the Muslim corsairs sent raiding and slave-taking parties to the coasts of Devon and Cornwall, carrying off men, women and children from coastal villages. In 1617 an entire fishing convoy returning from the New-foundland Banks to Dorset was captured by Barbary men-of-war, and in 1631 the corsairs raided Baltimore in Southern Ireland, taking over 100 slaves. Their most dramatic raid was that undertaken by the renegade Dutch priva-teer Jan Jansz (known as Murad Rais), who in 1627 sailed to Iceland and plundered Reykjavik, taking salted fish, hides and more than 400 captives.

While it soothed the consciences of the states of Europe to condemn the Barbary scourge, there is little doubt that they could have destroyed the menace had they chosen to take concerted action against them. The Barbary states, however, were a convenient tool in maintaining the balance of power in the Mediterranean. All the players in the game were aware of this, and all exploited the situa-tion. Actions against the Muslim corsairs by English fleets took place from time to time – in a celebrated engagement in 1671, for instance, Sir Edward Spragge burned an Algerian squadron at Bougie – but these were not followed up and were primarily designed to

impress upon the Barbary states the wisdom of entering into treaty agreements with the English. Treaties exempting English ships from harassment naturally meant that the corsairs' energies were directed towards vessels of other nationalities, thus damaging the trade of competitors. Other European nations acted with equal calculation. The French too signed treaties of friendship with the Barbary states, but they were also the biggest investors in the Christian corsairs, and secretly funded the building of ships in Malta to sail against the Muslims.

It was not until 1682 that an effective agreement was reached. By the terms of this treaty, English slaves were to be redeemed at the going rate, and English merchantmen were to sail unmolested, although the corsairs retained the right to board them and inspect their passes. Despite the numerous short-comings of the treaty, similar agreements were signed with Tripoli and Tunis, and over a period of time most English slaves gained their freedom. The agreement was several times amended and renewed, and was to last in essence for 150 years.

RIGHT: *In 1683 the French Consul Father Le Vacher and twenty other French residents of Algiers were seized by a mob and blown from the mouths of cannons in response to the French blockade of the port.*

ABOVE: *Lord Exmouth's representatives, Sir Charles Penrose and
Sir James Brisbane, in audience with the Dey of Algiers during
negotiations for the freeing of Christian slaves after the
bombardment of August 1816. The interpreter Abraham Salamé
gestures towards the British flagship* Queen Charlotte *in the
harbour.*

The growing strength of English and French maritime power led to a slow decline in the fortunes of the corsairs during the eighteenth century, and the Barbary states were forced to direct their attentions to the less powerful nations. The outbreak of war between England and France in 1793, however, saw a last burst of activity from the corsairs, who took full advantage of the chaos into which Europe was plunged. But with the end of the Napoleonic Wars in 1815 came a backlash of opinion against the corsairs, and their continued presence was seen as a calculated and unacceptable insult to European values and international security. In 1816 an Anglo-Dutch force bombarded Algiers and freed some 3,000 captives. The activities of the corsairs were not finally ended, however, until 1830 when Algiers was invaded by the French. The campaign established a permanent French colonial presence in Algiers, a presence which swiftly persuaded Tunis and Tripoli to renounce slavery and corsair activity. The story which had begun with the brothers Barbarossa three centuries before was thus brought to a close, and for the next century and more the coastal states of North Africa were controlled by the very same countries from which they had profited so handsomely for so long.

ABOVE: *Map of Asia from*
*Joan Blaeu's* Atlas Maior
*(11 volumes, Amsterdam,*
*1662-65).*

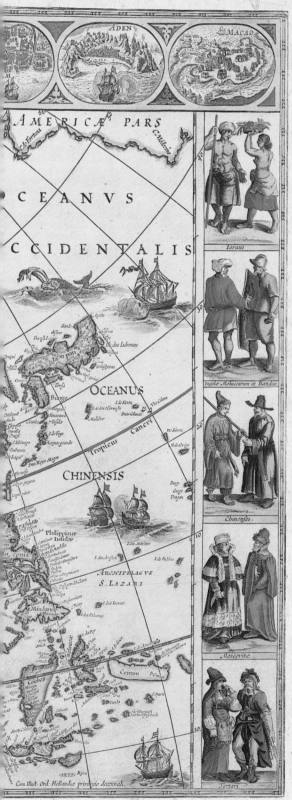

# A Gold Chain or a Wooden Leg

## PIRATES IN THE INDIAN OCEAN

**I**f trade followed the flag in the era of European expansion, piracy was never far behind, a persistent irritant snapping at the heels of legitimate commerce and snatching what takings it could. With the decline of Spanish power in the West Indies the great age of piracy in the Caribbean waned in the course of the seventeenth century; but new trading opportunities beckoned from the eastern seas, and the robbers who had preyed on the Spanish treasure galleons began to shift their unwelcome attentions to a new source of booty. The possible rewards were spectacular, as were the risks: and there were enough adventurous gamblers in whom the lust for gold outweighed the dangers to life and limb.

Native pirates had been plying the oceans beyond the Cape of Good Hope for centuries, and Marco Polo had recorded the dangers of piracy off the coasts of western India as early as 1290: each year from Gujarat and Malabar more than a hundred pirate craft cruised the waters in fleets of twenty to thirty vessels. They remained at sea the whole summer, taking their wives and children on the voyage. These fleets were strung out in what was called a 'sea-cordon' with about six miles between each ship. In this way they could quarter hundreds of square miles of ocean, snapping up merchant ships in their net. Of these pirates the most feared were the Gujarati rovers:

> THE PEOPLE ARE THE MOST DESPERATE PIRATES IN EXISTENCE, AND ONE OF THEIR ATROCITIES IS THIS: WHEN THEY HAVE TAKEN A MERCHANT VESSEL THEY FORCE THE MERCHANTS TO SWALLOW A STUFF CALLED TAMARINDI MIXED IN SEA-WATER, WHICH PRODUCES A VIOLENT PURGING. THIS IS DONE IN CASE THE MERCHANTS, ON SEEING THEIR DANGER, SHOULD HAVE SWALLOWED THEIR MOST VALUABLE STONES AND PEARLS. AND IN THIS WAY THE PIRATES SECURE THE WHOLE.

And other early travellers commented on the pirate ships infesting the oceans from the shores of the Red Sea to Celebes (Sulawesi) in South-East Asia. The arrival of European traders in substantial numbers in the early sixteenth century, however, introduced a new element into these centuries-old patterns of trade and plunder: as traders the Europeans provided a tempting new target for native pirates; in their turn they were often equally happy to steal from local merchant vessels encountered on their voyages. Justifying these

## PIRATES *of the* SILVER SCREEN

Hollywood and pirates seem to have been made for one another. From the earliest days of the silent screen, directors seized on pirates as a perfect vehicle for escapist adventure, romance in exotic locations and the use of stunning dramatic special effects and filmic sleights of hand.

One of the earliest triumphs was *The Black Pirate* (1926), in which Douglas Fairbanks Snr. starred as a young aristocrat who takes to piracy to avenge the death of his father. Filmed in experimental two-tone technicolor, it appeared to utilize a cast of thousands of cutlassed ruffians. Its high point came when Fairbanks climbed to the top of the mast, plunged his dagger into the main sail and abseiled down to the deck on it as the canvas cleaved.

It was feared that the advent of the 'talkies' would sound the death knell for these swashbuckling epics where action was all – a fight every ten minutes was the recommended formula – and dialogue seemed redundant. But in 1935 a remake of the silent 1924 film of *Captain Blood*, based on Rafael Sabatini's novel, made a

[ 68 ]

ABOVE LEFT:
*Errol Flynn plays a privateer sent by*
*Elizabeth I against the Spanish in* The Sea Hawk
*(1940)*. ABOVE RIGHT: The Black Pirate *(1926) was the*
*earliest of the cinematic pirate classics.*

star out of the unknown Errol Flynn as a wronged surgeon who turns pirate and ends up as Governor of Jamaica with Olivia de Havilland playing his bride. *Captain Blood* established Flynn as a swashbuckling devil-may-care hero.

In their heyday pirates of the silver screen were an idealized breed. Heroes played by actors like Fairbanks and Flynn were not ruthless villains, bloodthirsty for plunder. Rather they were outlaws with a mission, Robin Hoods of the waves, seeking to right a wrong or fight for a cause. Cinema audiences sat on the edge of their seats thrilling to the magnificent galleons, the pirates' daring exploits, their skilled swordsmanship, flashing, moustachioed smiles and frequently glimpsed torsos. But by the mid-1960s a new gritty realism had permeated the cinema, and what the new breed of heroes had on offer was no longer romantic escapism on the high seas.

acts of piracy was not difficult, for from the dawn of European expansion into the eastern oceans religious differences provided a convenient excuse to plunder the ships of other nations. Adherents of Islam stood outside the rules of Christian conduct, and were hence considered fair game for the Europeans. First on the scene were the Portuguese, and by the middle of the sixteenth century Portuguese merchants had established trading centres linking the east coast of Africa with the islands of South-East Asia. The early Portuguese travellers, edging round the coast of Africa towards the Indies, encountered an intricate web of trade controlled either by native merchants who wanted no interference, or by Arab merchants, who resented rivals trespassing on what they considered to be their preserve. The actions of these Europeans did not bode well for future relations. In 1498, Vasco da Gama, sailing to the east, violated any trust between the native traders and the European explorers when he plundered an Indian dhow off the African coast and stole a great store of gold and silver. He in turn became a target for local marauders, and was attacked by pirates sailing out of Goa in small brigantines hung with flags and streamers, the crew beating drums and sounding trumpets to intimidate their European enemies.

Vasco da Gama's rounding of the Cape of Good Hope in 1497 opened the sea route to the east. A century of Portuguese domination of the eastern seas followed, but increasing competition for these lucrative markets from the Dutch and the English eventually broke the Portuguese monopoly: by the early 1600s both England and Holland had founded trading companies with the aim of establishing commercial supremacy. Operating under the protection of government charters, these 'merchant adventurers' claimed a freedom of action in their pursuit of trade that would be unthinkable today. With aggressive attitudes

# PIRATE WEAPONS

The pirate was essentially an opportunist, and many of the necessities of life were taken from his victims. Medicines, food and ship's stores were all valuable plunder; weapons too might well be taken from the prey, and would therefore be no different from those in common use among seafarers: the musket, pistol, sword and boarding axe.

The popular image of the pirate, fostered in our own day by the swashbucklers of the Hollywood film, has the pirate armed with a rapier and fighting against fearsome odds. But most accounts indicate that, apart from encounters with military vessels, full-scale and bloody battles were the exception. For the merchant ship caught by a pirate, discretion was more often the better part of valour: to put up too fierce a fight would invite reprisals if the pirates eventually won the day, and after a token resistance the ship would more often be surrendered in exchange for the lives of the crew.

When there was a fight, the most popular ploys were stealth, surprise and trickery: the popular image of two large ships engaging in battle with broadsides is less common in reality, and both sides appear to have relied more often on small arms and hand weapons of various sorts.

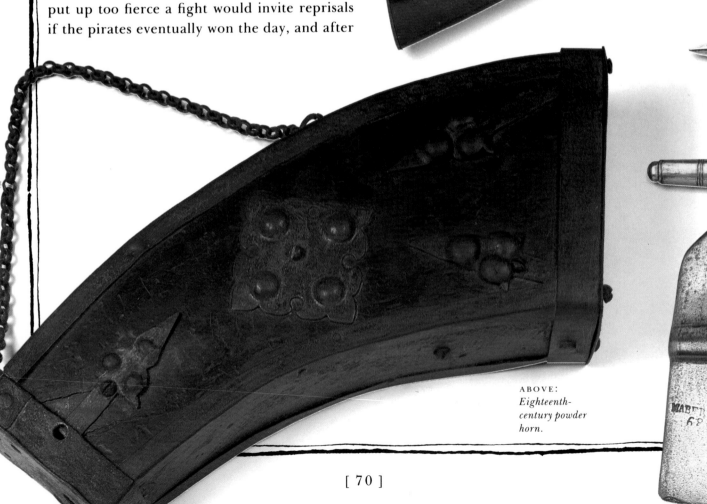

ABOVE:
*Eighteenth-century powder horn.*

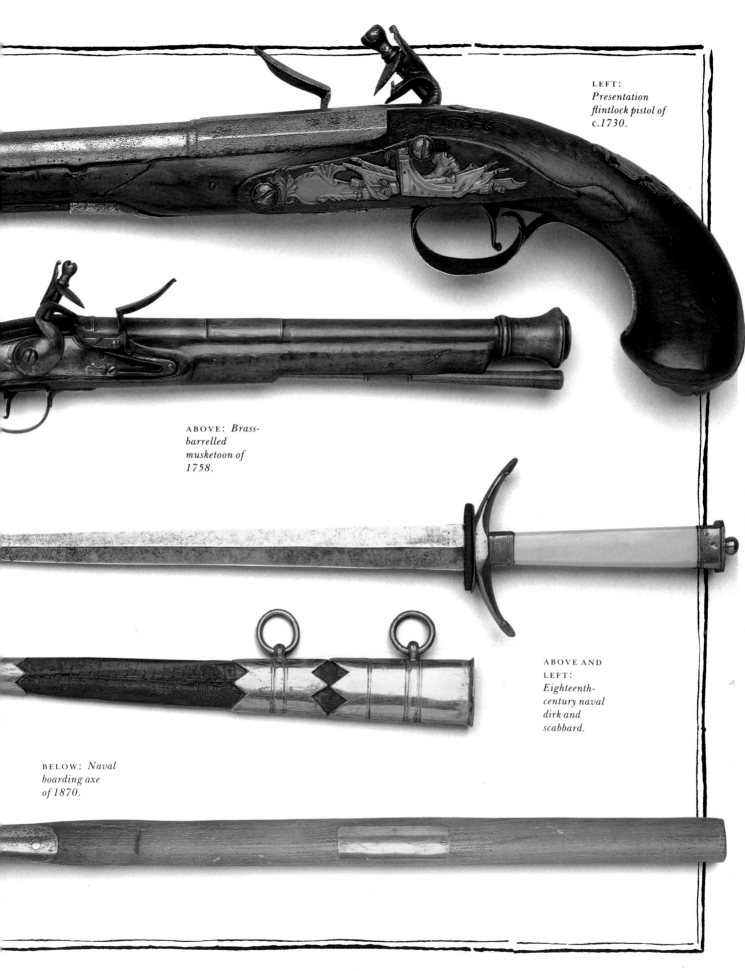

LEFT:
*Presentation
flintlock pistol of
c.1730.*

ABOVE: *Brass-
barrelled
musketoon of
1758.*

ABOVE AND
LEFT:
*Eighteenth-
century naval
dirk and
scabbard.*

BELOW: *Naval
boarding axe
of 1870.*

bolstered by an unshakeable sense of racial and religious superiority, these traders had no compunction in seizing the vessels both of native merchants and of their European rivals. Financing voyages to the east was expensive, and the goal of profit was paramount; and so while the East India Company had no formal policy on piracy in its early days, it was left largely to the discretion of individual commanders whether they took advantage of their size and armaments when richly-stocked native or hostile European vessels were encountered. Even the first voyage of the English East India Company in 1601, made by four ships under the command of James Lancaster, was more like a privateering attack upon Spanish and Portuguese trade than a genuine trading voyage. In early 1612 another Company commander, Sir Henry Middleton, who had been imprisoned by the authorities on the island of Socotra at the mouth of the Red Sea in 1609, seized and plundered two Portuguese ships at Dabhol in western India, before returning to the scene of his earlier humiliation, 'to revenge us of the wrongs offered us both by Turks and Mogols'. In May of the following year he met up with Captain John Saris, and together they proceeded to harass the native traders of the area. They poisoned trading relations for years to come by ransacking some fifteen native ships, forcing the owners to trade their goods for unwanted English broadcloth. Even a few ships acting in this way could disrupt trade out of all proportion to their strength, and by 1613 the Venetian ambassador at Constantinople was writing to his masters about the effects of these piracies, saying that a messenger had come from Cairo, 'sent express from the Pasha to report the great damage inflicted . . . in the Red Sea. Their constant plundering of rich Turkish ships is threatening the great city of Cairo with ruin to its trade.' However, the East India Company was now establishing per-

manent trading centres on the Indian mainland, and its dependence on the good-will of the Moghul authorities forced it to forbid such activities on the part of its commanders. Indeed, by the end of the seventeenth century, the Company had taken responsibility, albeit unwillingly, for the policing of the Indian Ocean.

The rival factions of English policy also used piracy to further their own interests and, by embroiling themselves in the already involved situation in the Indian Ocean, further complicated matters. While the East India Company attempted to distance itself from the illegal seizure of shipping, its efforts were being undermined by its own sovereign. In 1630 Charles I, habitually short of funds, granted a commission to Captain Richard Quail to cruise in the Red Sea and seize ships of 'any country that were not friends or allies of His Majesty'. Quail attacked several ships in the area and this frankly piratical expedition was a great success; it in turn gave the impetus to a further commission from the King to Captain William Cobb in 1635,

TO RANGE THE SEAS ALL OVER . . . AND TO MAKE PRIZE OF ALL SUCH TREASURES, MERCHANDISES . . . WHICH HE SHALL BE ABLE TO TAKE OF INFIDELS OR OF ANY OTHER PRINCE, POTENTATE OR STATE NOT IN LEAGUE OR AMITY WITH US BEYOND THE LINE EQUINOCTIAL [IE THE EQUATOR].

After Cobb's commission it became a popular saying amongst English seamen that there was 'no peace beyond the line'. Cobb took several Indian trading vessels in the Red Sea, bringing down the wrath of the Moghul authorities (already incensed by the actions of European interlopers in the area) on to the heads of the East India Company's representatives at Surat, their main trading post on the west coast of India. The English merchants were tortured

ABOVE: *Bow view of an East Indiaman, by Peter Monamy, c.1700.*

and imprisoned, and only finally gained their freedom after the Company had paid a ransom of £18,000. Although the East India Company pressed to have Cobb tried in England for piracy, his friends in high places ensured that the case dragged on inconclusively until 1644. The anger of the Indian authorities is not hard to understand, and is echoed again and again in official dealings relating to the growth of the pirate menace. The Company in turn had the tricky task of trying to explain how it was that English ships, licensed by the King of England, had no connection with the East India Company, even though the trading charter of that company was granted by the same sovereign.

The embarrassment caused to the East India Company by Cobb's voyage was not entirely unwelcome to his sponsors, a group of merchants who shortly afterwards obtained a charter from the King giving them equal rights to trade in the east. The Courteen Association, named after its wealthy backer Sir William Courteen, was one of several groups who at one time or another tried to carve out a slice of the Company's markets. This competition died away, but not before a disastrous attempt had been made by supporters of the Courteen Association to colonize the island of Madagascar as a foothold in the Indian Ocean. The project, poorly conceived and incompetently executed, cost the lives of several hundred settlers lured by the descriptions of Madagascar as 'the richest and most fruitful island in the world'. This scheme was widely derided at the time, particularly by the East India Company, which saw the threat to its monopoly of English trade in the Indian Ocean, but had it been successful it might well have denied the pirates of the Indian Ocean the secure and safe haven that they enjoyed in Madagascar in the later years of the century (see pp. 82–3).

## THE BUCCANEERS ARRIVE

By 1671 the East India Company's own ships were threatened by pirates to the extent that its President at Surat was offering a handsome incentive to privateers to seek out pirates, rewarding them with a third of the booty taken from any captured ship. But this action (which echoed a similar act of the English Parliament in 1642) did little to stem the menace, which inevitably kept pace with the growth of trade. By the 1670s the whole Indian Ocean littoral, from the Red Sea to the south-western shores of the Indian sub-continent, had become a pirate coast. In addition to the Malabar pirates of the west coast, there were the growing

# THE ATTACK

Pirate ships have ranged in size from the 600-ton war junks of the Chinese pirates and the oared galleys of the Barbary corsairs to the native canoes used by the pirates of Indonesia. But pirate tactics have invariably relied on speed, surprise or terror to achieve the objective.

One of the most graphic accounts of a pirate action can be found in the journal of Basil Ringrose, who spent two years in the company of Captain Bartholomew Sharp and other buccaneers plundering ships and villages around the coast of Central and South America. On 23 April 1680 a group of buccaneers came up against three Spanish warships off Panama City. The buccaneers, who were in canoes taken from the local Indians, immediately rowed to windward of the largest ship. Using their long-barrelled muskets they shot the helmsman and the crew working the sails, causing the ship to fall away from the wind with her sails aback. Firing continuously the buccaneers rowed up under the ship's stern and with further accurate shots cut through the mainsheet and the brace, which were the ropes controlling the mainsail. Finally they wedged the rudder so that the ship was totally disabled.

When the buccaneers climbed on board they found two-thirds of the crew dead. The remainder surrendered and the buccaneers went on to capture the other two ships. At the end of the action the band of sixty-eight buccaneers had lost eighteen men killed. The 228 men in the Spanish warships on the other hand, taken by surprise by the attack, had been unable to make effective use of their cannon and had lost sixty-one killed and many more wounded.

On this occasion the buccaneers relied on the speed and boldness of their attack, the ability of their canoes to out-manoeuvre the sailing ships, and the accuracy of their shooting. Pirates also used deception to catch their victims off guard. The most common ploy was to fly the flags of a friendly or neutral nation when approaching the intended prize. Ropes were sometimes dragged behind the pirate ship to slow her down and give the impression of a heavily laden merchant ship. At the last minute the false flags were hauled down and replaced by the skull and crossbones, and the pirates who had been hiding below deck

RIGHT: *Pirates dressed as women attempt to decoy a merchantman in this fanciful engraving by the nineteenth-century French artist Auguste-François Biard.*

BELOW LEFT: *The American illustrator Howard Pyle shows buccaneers in small boats attacking a Spanish galleon from the stern.*

opened fire and rapidly boarded their prey. The terrified crew of the merchant ship, taken by surprise, usually surrendered without a fight.

One of the most ingenious deceptions was carried out by Henry Morgan at Maracaibo on the South American coast in 1669. Trapped inside the lagoon by three Spanish warships, he disguised a captured merchant ship as his flagship. Gun ports were cut in her sides and fitted with hollow logs for guns, and the decks were lined with pieces of wood painted and dressed to look like seamen. Twelve buc-caneers then sailed the ship towards the flag-ship of the Spanish squadron which prepared to engage the enemy. Just before coming alongside the buccaneers lit fuses attached to barrels of gunpowder and escaped in small boats. The disguised merchant ship exploded and set fire to the Spanish flagship which had to be abandoned by her crew. Morgan's fleet managed to escape with one of the Spanish ships as a prize.

BELOW: *A view of Surat, the East India Company's first permanent trading settlement in the Indian sub-continent, from the sea in 1673.*

bands of Sanganian pirates from Gujarat to the north, vicious and merciless robbers who drugged themselves before going into battle, and presented a frightening spectacle to their foes with their long hair let down to indicate they would give no quarter to any prisoners they took. To the west, the Omani Arab pirates had also become a force to be reckoned with by the mid-seventeenth century. They struck a decisive blow to the already stagnating

Portuguese power, and in 1650 took Muscat, the last remaining Portuguese base of any consequence in the area. The arrival in the last quarter of the seventeenth century of bands of English adventurers, sailing 'on the account' from the West Indies, introduced a new measure of violence and criminality to Indian waters. (By the use of the language of the book-keeper, the pirates ironically became part of the trading network: those engaged in piracy considered themselves as on the account, while captured booty was invariably termed 'purchase'.)

English buccaneers and pirates had been drawn irresistibly to the West Indies by the huge wealth of the Spanish empire. Spain was

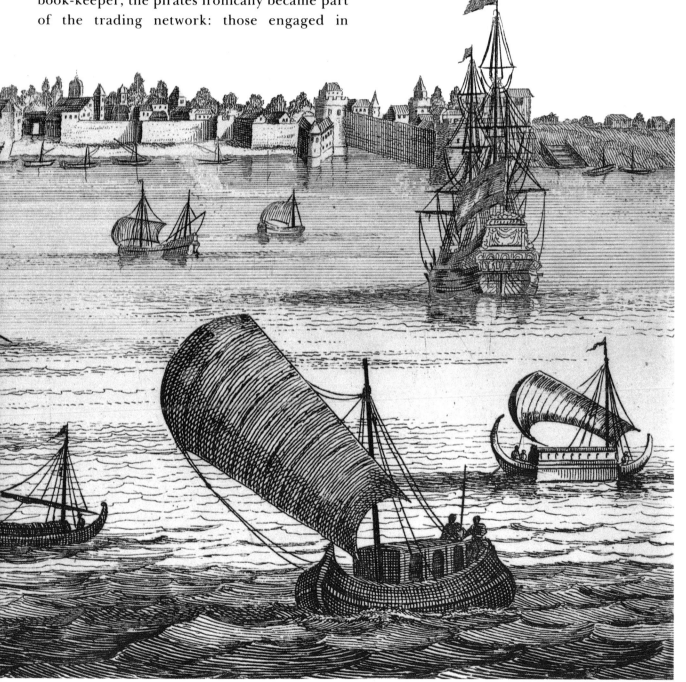

# THE PIRATE FLAG

The hero of Daniel Defoe's novel *Captain Singleton*, commanding a pirate ship in the Indian Ocean in the early eighteenth century, records various flags flown before an action: 'a black flag with two cross daggers in it on our mainmast head', and also 'the black flag or ancient in the poop and the bloody flag at the topmast head'. While it is the black flag which is most commonly associated with pirates today, the red flag – a signal that no quarter would be given in battle – is of greater antiquity and was as widespread during the great age of piracy. It is this red flag that supplies what is perhaps the most likely derivation of 'Jolly Roger', from the French 'Joli Rouge'. English pirates, taking it to mean the pirate flag in general, may then have transferred an anglicized version of the name to the black flag which came into common use in the early eighteenth century.

The skull and crossbones, often seen on tombstones and an immediately recognizable symbol of death, was a natural image to strike fear into a pirate's victims, and its use with a black flag dates from about the end of the seventeenth century. It seems to have evolved

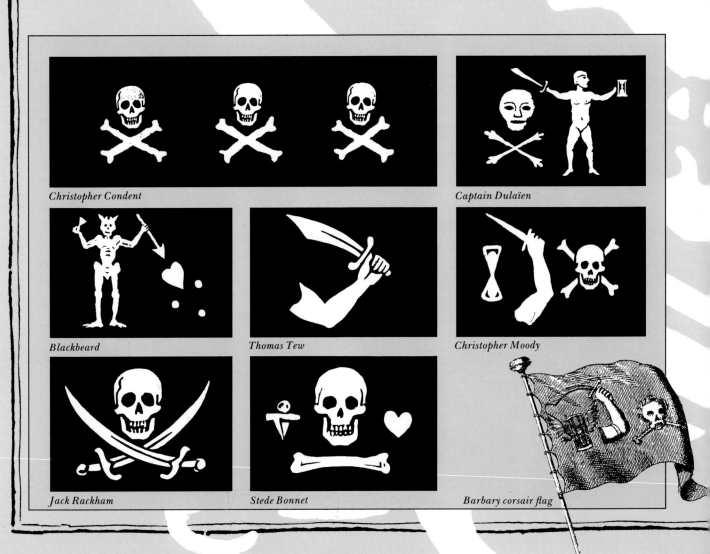

Christopher Condent

Captain Dulaïen

Blackbeard

Thomas Tew

Christopher Moody

Jack Rackham

Stede Bonnet

Barbary corsair flag

ABOVE: *The flamboyant Bartholomew
Roberts, shown here at Whydah on the
Guinea Coast in 1722 with two of his ships,
the* Royal Fortune *and the* Ranger.

from a more complicated symbolic design incorporating other motifs: in 1700 Captain Cranby of HMS *Poole* records that the French pirate Emmanuel Wynne fought under 'a sable ensign with crossbones, a Death's head and an hour glass'.

Similarly, a group of pirates hanged at Newport, Rhode Island in 1723 sailed under a flag on which was a skeleton, 'with an hour glass in one hand and a dart in the heart and three drops of blood proceeding from it in the other . . . Which flag they called Old Roger and often used to say they would live and die under it'.

In a letter of 1724 Captain Richard Hawkins, who was captured by pirates, gives the first recorded instance of the present name, and reminds us that the black flag would have been a more welcome sight than the red: '[his cap-

tors] hoisted Jolly Roger . . . in the middle of which is a large white skeleton with a dart in one hand, striking a bleeding heart, and in the other an hour glass . . . When they fight under Jolly Roger, they give quarter, which they do not when they fight under the red or bloody flag.'

The standard skull and crossbones could be altered to suit individual whim, and the basic design was probably elaborated on by many pirate captains. It is known that Bartholomew Roberts, for instance, angered by the repeated attempts of the governors of Barbados and Martinique to capture him, ordered a new flag to be made for his ship, 'with his own figure portrayed, standing upon two skulls, and under them the letters ABH and AMH, signifying A Barbadian's Head and A Martinican's Head'.

the historic enemy of England and so these predatory raids for easy riches could be combined with a comforting sense of patriotic duty. Acting with the open or tacit encouragement of their government the English pirates' depredations could be presented as the actions of servants of the Crown. While the buccaneers and filibusters plundered on their own account, they had also formed a useful quasi-official mercenary force in the protection of the early English and French settlements in the West Indies against the might of Spain. But with the decline of Spanish power in the New World, the rich pickings of former years disappeared, and these anarchic bands became a nuisance to be stamped out. A proportion settled into the planting or trading communities of the West Indian islands, while others were absorbed into the navies of various European powers. But for those unruly or simply adventurous spirits for whom such activities were too tame, the lure of the Indian Ocean proved irresistible, and they sailed east to swell the numbers of an already thriving pirate community. As Lord Bellomont, Governor of New York, wrote to the Admiralty in 1699: 'The vast riches of the Red Sea and Madagascar are such a lure to seamen that there's almost no withholding them from turning pirate'. An added attraction was the lack of any strong naval power to police the oceans beyond the Cape.

Many of these pirates from the European settlements of North America and the West Indies were privateers with commissions from local governors against national enemies. Even though their real purpose of piracy was evident to all, a blind eye was turned to these activities which handsomely profited the local economy. Most of the buccaneers came to the Indian Ocean *via* the Cape of Good Hope, although some made their way from the Pacific by way of the Spanish settlements in South-

East Asia. Numerous adventurers also came from the west coast of Africa, where frequent mutinies amongst the crews of merchant ships swelled the ranks of freebooters eager to find out for themselves the truth of persistent rumours of the easy pickings east of the Cape. As they rounded the Cape they found a ready jumping off point in the island of Madagascar – a convenient base for intercepting the east-bound Indian trade and for cruising off Red Sea waters. From Madagascar the pirate fleets scoured the eastern seas, loitering at the mouth of the Red Sea in wait for the richly laden pilgrim ships plying between Gujarat and Mecca, and roving as far east as the Bay of Bengal and even Sumatra in search of prey. Returning to the pirate communities in Madagascar they could lie up, repair their ships, and carouse and barter with the merchants who flocked to St Mary's Island to trade in stolen goods. Although no more than several hundred pirates can have settled on Madagascar at any one time, the mystery of the island (little-known despite its size), its exotic reputation and the absence of other European settlers caused it to be seen as a 'pirate island' in the popular imagination. Soon stories of pirate chiefs living in tropical splendour and ruling whole tribes of natives began to filter back to Europe, endowing the pirates with a lifestyle and riches few of them can have known.

## PLUNDERING
## THE WEALTH OF
## THE INDIES

There were, without doubt, large catches to be made in the ocean trade of the eastern seas. But in order to chase such wealth the pirate had also to capture more mundane booty. The necessities of life were always needed – food-stuffs, medicine, carpenter's tools, rope and rigging, weapons and gunpowder. And unlike

ABOVE: *Pirates clearing the decks of an
East Indiaman. An imaginative, if
somewhat stylized, American mid-
nineteenth century reconstruction, from
Charles Ellms'* The pirates own book
*(Philadelphia, 1844).*

the legitimate trader, the pirate could not put
into port for replenishment and repairs. Hard
usage and the ravages of the teredos worm
soon made a vessel unseaworthy in tropical
waters, and as often as not it was the victim's
ship itself that was most needed. Indian trade
with the Red Sea was paid for in gold and
silver, and these universal currencies were thus
the treasure for which the pirates fought. The
disposal of other kinds of merchandise was
often more complicated. The ideal was to take
an East Indiaman on its outward voyage when
it was carrying gold and silver to buy cargo. In
addition to ready money, an outward-bound
ship was loaded with provisions of food and
drink 'and great quantities of the like sent to
the governors and factories at the English
settlements'. Ships plundered on the return
journey, however, were often loaded with
bulky cargoes of silks and spices that could not
be easily stored on the small pirate vessel, and
which were often difficult to dispose of. And
when the booty could be sold, it invariably
went at a discount to those traders (such as the
merchant ships that flocked to Madagascar)
who knew they were dealing in stolen goods.
This in part explains the profligate extravagance of so many pirates. The traveller John
Ovington describes a pirate band in 1689 who
replaced their worn-out canvas sails with
double silk and who were 'so frank both in
distributing their goods, and guzzling down
the noble wine, as if they were both wearied
with the possession of their rapine, and willing

# MADAGASCAR:
*the pirate island*

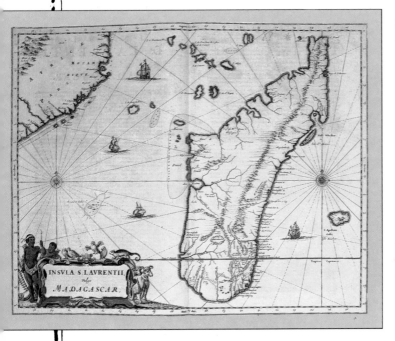

notorious pirates in the world, including Captain William Kidd, Thomas White, Captain England and that 'wicked and ill-disposed person' Thomas Tew.

The lives of these men, living in supposed ease and luxury on a wild and tropical isle, gave rise to fantastic stories of pirate kingdoms beyond the reach of the laws of Europe and funded by the immense wealth of ill-gotten gains. But in reality much of these riches – silks, spices, jewels – were funnelled straight back to Europe and America by traders who in their turn were only too willing to prey on the pirates, flocking to their hideaways (under the pretence of the more respectable trade of slave-gathering) to provide them with the basic necessities of life at hugely inflated prices.

For some thirty years between 1690 and 1720 the immense island of Madagascar, lying off the eastern seaboard of Africa, was the principal base of pirates preying on the rich trade of the Indian Ocean.

Uncolonized and barely explored beyond the coastal fringes, Madagascar was an ideal bolthole for the pirates driven out of the Caribbean in the closing years of the seventeenth century. They were drawn in greatest numbers to St Mary's Island on the north-east coast which, with its fine, easily fortified harbour, became a *rendezvous* for pirates returning from forays into the Indian Ocean. A visitor at the end of the seventeenth century counted 17 pirate vessels and an estimated population of 1500 men. At various times the island was to play host to many of the most

ABOVE: *A nineteenth-century fantasy of
the imagined ease and tropical pleasures
of life in the pirate haven of
Madagascar.*

## REASONS

For Reducing the

### Pyrates at Madagaſcar:

AND

**PROPOSALS** *humbly offered to the Honourable Houſe of Commons, for effecting the ſame.*

THAT certain Pyrates having ſome Years ſince found the Iſland of *Madagaſcar* to be the moſt Proper, if not the only Place in the World for their Abode, and carrying on their Deſtructive Trade with Security, betook themſelves thither; and being ſince increaſed to a formidable Body are become a manifeſt Obſtruction to Trade, and Scandal to our Nation and Religion, being moſt of them *Engliſh*, at leaſt four Fifths.

That *Madagaſcar* is one of the Largeſt Iſlands in the World, and very Fruitful, lies near the Entrance into the *Eaſt-Indies*, and is divided into a great many petty Kingdoms independant of each other, ſo that there is no making Application to any Supream Monarch (or indeed any elſe) to Expel or Deſtroy the Pyrates there.

That upon a general Peace, when Multitudes of Soldiers and Seamen will wantEmployment; or by length of Time, and the Pyrates generating with the Women of the Country, their Numbers ſhould be increaſed, they may form themſelves into a Settlement of Robbers, as Prejudicial to Trade as any on the Coaſt of *Affrica*.

For it's natural to conſider, That all Perſons owe by Inſtinct a Love to the Place of their Birth: Therefore the preſent Pyrates muſt deſire to return to their Native Country; and if this preſent Generation ſhould be once Extinct, their Children will have the ſame Inclination to *Madagaſcar* as theſe have to *England*, and will not have any ſuch Affection for *England*, altho' they will retain the Name of *Engliſh*; and conſequently all thoſe ſucceeding Depredations committed by them will be charged to the Account of *England*. Notwithſtanding they were not born with us, ſo that this ſeems the only Time for Reducing them to their Obedience, and preventing all thoſe evil Conſequences.

It muſt therefore be allow'd to be a very deſirable and neceſſary Thing, that they ſhould be ſuppreſſed in Time; and that if it ever be effected, it muſt be either by Force or Perſwaſion.

ABOVE: *This broadsheet of about 1705 argued that the pirates were so firmly entrenched in Madagascar that the only practical solution to the problem was to offer them 'a gracious and free pardon.*

splendour that Plantain found himself 'at a loss how to behave himself, having been so used to a brutish way of living at Madagascar'.

By the early eighteenth century the years of pirate power on the island were over. When the English privateer Captain Woodes Rogers was at the Cape in 1711 he was told by two ex-pirates who had spent some years in Madagascar that only 60 or 70 pirates remained, and that they, far from reigning as kings in a tropical paradise, lived in squalor and distress, 'most of them very poor and despicable, even to the natives'. In 1719 the East Indiaman *St George* visited St Mary's, and found the dispirited remnants of the pirate John Halsey's company, some 17 men worn down by the tedium of exile, who 'wanted but one hit more and then to go home, for they were aweary of their course of life'. The final irony of their situation was that a general pardon had in fact been issued to pirates by the British government the previous year.

BELOW: *Letter signed by Abraham Samuel, 'King of Port Dolphin', regarding the sale of the pirate ship* Prophet Daniel, *dated 31 October 1699.*

From this rich trade there arose the myth of the pirate kings that gained such widespread currency in England. But such stories were largely fantasy: while 'King' Samuel at Port Dauphin certainly existed, his authority extended over only a small area of the island. James Plantain, self-proclaimed King of Ranter Bay to the north of St Mary's, had pretensions to greater power, and dressed his numerous Madagascan wives in English clothes, decking them with jewels and giving them names such as Moll, Kate, Sue and Pegg. But like so many of the Madagascar pirates, Plantain's end was obscure. He is reputed to have ended his days in the service of the great Indian pirate Angria, who lived in such

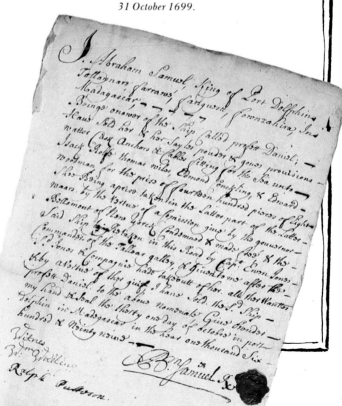

to stifle all the melancholy reflections concerning it'. Clement Downing, who visited Madagascar with the anti-piracy squadron of Thomas Mathews in 1722, vividly portrayed a scene of waste and extravagance in an image that sums up the futility of so much of the pirate's life:

... THIS MOOR'S SHIP HAD MORE VALUE IN DIAMONDS, RUBIES, AND EMERALDS, WITH THE RICHEST OF DRUGS, AND A GREAT QUANTITY OF BALM OF GILEAD; ALL WHICH THESE PYRATES MADE WASTE OF, AND SUFFERED THE SAME TO LIE EXPOSED TO THE WIND AND WEATHER ON THE ISLAND OF ST MARY. THERE WE FOUND THE RUINS OF SEVERAL SHIPS AND THEIR CARGOES PILED UP IN GREAT HEAPS, CONSISTING OF THE RICHEST SPICES AND DRUGS; ALL WHICH THEY VALUED NOT: BUT MONEY, RICH SILKS, DIAMONDS, AND OTHER JEWELS, THEY TOOK CARE OF; AND ALL EATABLES AND DRINKABLES WHICH THEY FANCIED ...

But the rewards in ready currency could be huge even after these useless luxuries had been discarded. Adam Baldridge, trading with the pirates at St Mary's Island off Madagascar, reported that in 1691 the pirate George Raynor arrived in port after taking an Indian ship in the Red Sea. So great was the haul that each man of his crew received £1,100 as his share, more than an honest seaman could hope to earn in a lifetime. Although such takings were exceptional, they occurred often enough to swell the number of pirates willing to risk all in pursuit of such bounty. The voyage of Thomas Tew, in particular, drew adventurers to the seemingly infinite wealth of the Indies. Tew had originally set out with a privateering commission from the Governor of the Bermudas to harass the French trading post at Goree on the west coast of Africa. The pros-

pect of small returns and a considerable risk grew less appealing as the seamen neared their destination, and Tew persuaded his crew to turn pirate and head for the Red Sea, offering them the chance of 'a gold chain or a wooden leg' in their pursuit of wealth. In the summer of 1693 they took one of the Moghul's ships *en route* between Jeddah and Surat and, after torturing their captives for six days to reveal the whereabouts of the treasure, made off with a haul that gave each man £1,200. A single action, in which none of his men had been injured, had netted a fortune, and Tew's return to a hero's welcome in Newport in 1694 further inflamed the greed of those who saw the results of his voyage.

Few outlets for conspicuous consumption – apart from liquor and debauchery – existed in the pirate hideouts, and much of their stolen wealth was taken back to be sold in the major ports of the American seaboard, either shipped by traders from Madagascar, or brazenly brought back by the pirates themselves as they returned from their forays to the east. As long as palms were greased sufficiently generously, few questions were asked about the origins of these riches, and in 1696, two years after Tew's homecoming, Governor Fletcher could write: 'Rhode Island is now a free port for pirates. Thomas Tew ... brought there £100,000 from the Red Sea in 1694'. But Tew for one was not to enjoy his wealth for long. Although Fletcher had described him as a pirate, he seems to have been untroubled by the morality of Tew's actions, and it did not prevent him commissioning him once more, this time against the French in Canada. Tew again set sail for the east (for Canada *via* the Red Sea!) at the end of 1694. There he joined the notorious Henry Avery and in September 1695 was killed while boarding an Indian trading ship. Captain Johnson in his *General history of the ... Pirates* takes a certain grim pleasure in spelling out the perils of piracy and its rewards:

> IN THE ENGAGEMENT A SHOT CARRIED AWAY THE RIM OF TEW'S BELLY, WHO HELD HIS BOWELS WITH HIS HANDS SOME SMALL SPACE. WHEN HE DROPPED, IT STRUCK SUCH TERROR IN HIS MEN THAT THEY SUFFERED THEM-SELVES TO BE TAKEN WITHOUT MAKING RESISTANCE.

At first the European pirates had restricted themselves to attacking native vessels, and indeed from time to time self-righteously proclaimed their patriotism. The pirate Henry Avery left a message at the island of Johanna off Madagascar in 1695, which declared that 'I have never as yet wronged any English or Dutch nor ever intend whilst I am commander', signing himself half-cajolingly and half-threateningly, as 'yet an Englishman's friend'. As time went by, however, and the seas became crowded with pirates, the temptation to attack European ships of other nationalities, and finally their own countrymen, proved too great to resist. In 1689 the authorities at Fort St George (Madras) reported that the sea trade was 'pestered with pirates', and despite harsh punishment the situation was little improved in the following years. Admiralty jurisdiction to try pirates had been granted to the East India Company in 1683, and hanging at the yard-arm, flogging round all the ships at anchor, and branding the letter 'P' with an iron stamp plunged in the flames, all became standard punishments, often meted out in an arbitrary way. Thus in 1690 the court at Fort St George records the fate of a band of pirates sent for trial, all of whom were found 'equally guilty, but in consideration of the small execution they had done, and that Justice is inclined to mercy, the Court thought fit to sentence two to death as well for example as Terror sake, taking the fortune of the dice, the rest to be

branded [with the letter P] in the forehead at the execution post'. The gallows or the branding post were suitably brutal punishments for men who were no strangers to violence and

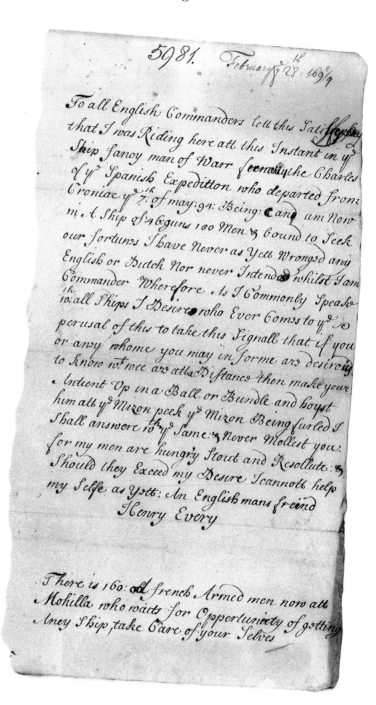

ABOVE: *A contemporary copy of a letter from Henry Avery, left on the island of Johanna off Madagascar, professing his patriotism and his determination not to attack English ships.*

# TRIALS *and* EXECUTIONS

In England and her colonies overseas the standard punishment for men convicted of piracy was death by hanging. In London this always took place at Execution Dock at Wapping, a few miles downstream from London Bridge. The convicted pirates were taken from the Marshalsea Prison or Newgate in a procession led by an officer carrying a silver oar symbolizing the authority of the High Court of the Admiralty. A wooden gallows was erected on the foreshore at the low-tide mark, enabling a huge crowd to watch the spectacle from the north bank of the Thames or from ships and boats moored out in the river. Standing on the platform with the rope around their necks, the pirates had to endure a sermon from the chaplain before being allowed to address the crowds. The last words of pirates were often printed and were always much in demand. After the execution had taken place the bodies were left until three tides had passed over them.

In 1701 an Act of Parliament authorized Vice-Admiralty Courts to be held in the colonies where the conduct of the trials and the executions followed a remarkably similar pattern to those held in England. In 1704, for instance, John Quelch and twenty-four pirates were put on trial at Boston. They had mutinied, taken over their ship, hoisted the pirate flag, and plundered nine Portuguese ships laden with gold and silver. After a lengthy show trial, seven pirates including Quelch were taken from the gaol to the water-front, behind an officer bearing the silver oar. They were then rowed across the harbour to a small island, accompanied by the Reverend Cotton Mather. Judge Sewall noted in his diary:

WHEN I CAME TO SEE HOW THE RIVER WAS COVER'D WITH PEOPLE, I WAS AMAZED. SOME SAY THERE WERE 100 BOATS . . . WHEN THE SCAFFOLD WAS HOISTED TO A DUE HEIGHT, THE SEVEN MALEFACTORS WENT UP. MR MATHER PRAYED FOR THEM STANDING UPON THE BOAT. ROPES WERE FASTENED TO THE GALLOWS. WHEN THE SCAFFOLD WAS LET TO SINK THERE WAS SUCH A SCREECH OF THE WOMEN THAT MY WIFE HEARD IT SITTING IN HER ENTRY NEXT THE ORCHARD AND WAS MUCH SURPRISED BY IT.

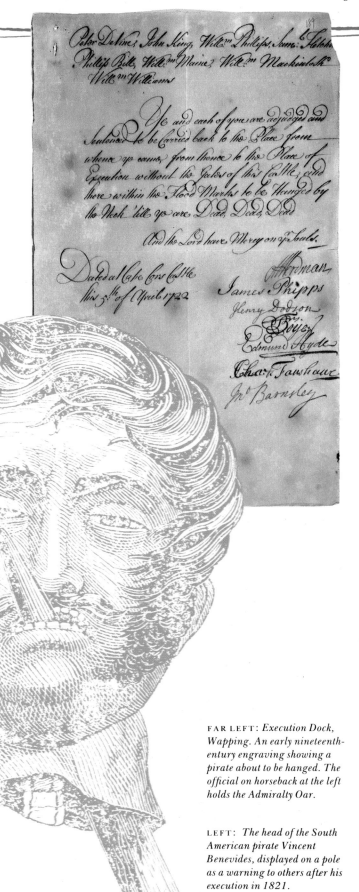

Peter Deline, John King, Will.m Phillips, Sam.ll Fletcher, Phillip Bell, Will.m Maine, Will.m Mackintosh, Will.m Williams

Ye and each of you are adjudged and sentenced to be carried back to the Place from whence yo came, from thence to the Place of Execution without the Gates of this Castle, and there within the Flood Marks to be Hanged by the Neck 'till yo are Dead, Dead, Dead

And the Lord have Mercy on yr Souls.

Dated at Cape Cors Castle this 5th of April 1722

Aldnman, James Phipps, Henry Dodson, Boye, Edmund Hyde, Cha.s Fanshaw, Jn.o Barnsley

*LEFT: The death sentence passed on eight men convicted of piracy in 1722.*

*RIGHT: The Admiralty Oar. The silver oar symbolized the authority of the High Court of Admiralty, and was carried in procession at the execution of pirates.*

*FAR LEFT: Execution Dock, Wapping. An early nineteenth-century engraving showing a pirate about to be hanged. The official on horseback at the left holds the Admiralty Oar.*

*LEFT: The head of the South American pirate Vincent Benevides, displayed on a pole as a warning to others after his execution in 1821.*

Most of the pirate trials were well documented and provide interesting information about the defendants and their crimes. In 1723 Captain Harris and his crew of pirates were tried by the Court of Vice Admiralty at Newport, Rhode Island. Of the thirty-five men on trial, fifteen were born in England, two in Ireland, three in Wales and the rest in North America. The average age of the crew was twenty-six. This follows the pattern of naval crews of the period, and underlines the fact that the handling of a sailing ship with constant sail changes and dangerous work aloft required a crew who were young, fit and strong.

The verdict at the end of this trial was that twenty of the pirates were found guilty and were hanged. Only ten were reprieved. The high proportion executed reflects the concern of the authorities at this time to stamp out piracy at all costs. In the previous century pardons were frequently issued to pirates, and according to Henry Mainwaring's observations on piracy written in 1617, the usual practice was that 'none but the Captain, Master, and it may be some few of the principal of the Company shall be put to death'.

intimidation, but the aura of romance still clung to those outstanding villains who by their daring seized great prizes and eluded the hangman's noose.

## HENRY AVERY: THE CREATION OF A LEGEND

Of all the European pirates who hunted the Indian seas it was Henry Avery (also known as John Every and Bridgeman) who was to become a figure of popular legend in the early eighteenth century. By 1695 Avery had built up a small fleet of ships, and in September they sighted two vessels of the Mocha fleet returning to Surat with pilgrims and a rich store of treasure. The smaller ship, the *Fateh Muhammad*, was taken with little difficulty and yielded some £40,000 of gold and silver. The greater prize was still ahead, and the pirates went in hot pursuit of the *Gang-i-Sawai*, catching up with her on 28 September only thirty miles off Surat. Despite mounting forty guns and carrying some 800 men, she appears to have capitulated after only a token resistance: one account states that the captain, having dressed the women on board in men's clothes and exhorted them to fight bravely, then fled below and hid with his officers. The *Gang-i-Sawai*, it transpired, belonged to the Moghul and was the largest Indian ship trading out of Surat, carrying pilgrims and merchandise each

*Below: Captain Avery taking treasure from the Indian ship* Gang-i-Sawai *on board the* Fancy *in September 1695. The value of the haul may have been as much as £325,000.*

ABOVE: *Persistent attacks on Indian pirates in the Persian*
*trade by Wahabi Gulf resulted in an English expedition*
*against their bases in 1809-10. This view shows the sacking*
*of the pirate headquarters of Ras al Khaymah on*
*13 November 1809.*

year to Mecca. As the value of their prize
dawned on the pirates, greed and lust over-
came them: passengers were tortured to reveal
the whereabouts of their valuables, many of
the women were raped, while others threw
themselves into the sea to escape dishonour.
Avery later denied these allegations, but the
final confession of John Sparcks, before his
death at Execution Dock in 1696, is more convincing. He referred specifically to the taking
of the *Gang-i-Sawai*, and

EXPRESSED A DUE SENSE OF HIS WICKED LIFE,
IN PARTICULAR TO THE MOST HORRID BAR-
BARITIES HE HAD COMMITTED, WHICH
THOUGH UPON THE PERSONS OF HEATHENS
AND INFIDELS, SUCH AS THE FOREMENTIONED
POOR INDIANS, SO INHUMANELY RIFLED AND

TREATED SO UNMERCIFULLY, DECLARING . . .
THAT HE JUSTLY SUFFERED DEATH FOR
SUCH INHUMANITY.

Estimates vary as to the value of the haul taken
from the *Gang-i-Sawai*, but it may have been as
much as £325,000, which would have given
each man nearly £2,000.

The Moghul Emperor reacted with fury to
the seizure of his ship, and his advisers had the
greatest difficulty in dissuading him from
immediately sacking the English settlements at
Bombay and Madras and repudiating all trade
agreements. Wiser counsel prevailed, however,
and after a period of imprisonment the
English traders at Surat were freed. But
Avery's continued raids led to further

# WILLIAM KIDD:
*Pirate Chaser
turned Pirate*

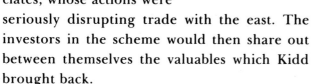

Many pirates ended their days at the end of a rope. Few, however, can have been so relentlessly pursued by bad luck as William Kidd, a successful New York businessman and ex-privateer who was persuaded by a powerful private syndicate to command a pirate-hunting expedition to the Indian Ocean against John Avery and his associates, whose actions were seriously disrupting trade with the east. The investors in the scheme would then share out between themselves the valuables which Kidd brought back.

But from the very beginning of the cruise misfortune was never far away. Half of Kidd's original crew were lost to the press-gang, and in September 1696 the *Adventure Galley* set sail from New York with a company recruited from the dregs of the waterfront, 'men of desperate fortunes and necessities', thirsty for treasure and with few scruples about how they obtained it.

The stresses of commanding a ship crewed by pirates in all but name told on Kidd, and his behaviour became increasingly aggressive and erratic. He appears soon to have given up all attempt at remaining within the law, attacking several obviously non-piratical vessels while still maintaining that he was acting according to his instructions. The threat became reality when, in October 1697, Kidd struck and killed a crew member, William Moore.

At this point Kidd appears to have decided that the mutinous grumbles of his crew were a more immediate threat to him than the authorities. In January 1698 he seized the *Quedah Merchant*, whose cargo he later sold for £10,000. Kidd would probably not have known that the Nine Years War against France had just ended, and since this ship carried a pass from the French East India Company, he was to argue that he.had taken her as a legal prize. But in fact the *Quedah Merchant* was an Armenian-owned vessel commanded by an English master. It was common practice for trading vessels to obtain passes from all the authorities operating in a given area: since

LEFT: *Kidd's privateering commission, issued under the authority of King William III.*

ABOVE: *A supposed portrait of Captain Kidd by an unknown artist.*

they took Kidd's to be a French ship, they had shown him a French pass. Kidd took her to the pirate base of St Mary's Island, Madagascar, where he fatally compromised himself by swearing fidelity to the pirate Robert Culliford. He then prepared to return to America, having taken no pirates, but apparently still believing that he could justify his acts under the guise of privateering. On his arrival, however, he was arrested by the Governor of New York, his former sponsor Lord Bellomont, and shipped back to England for trial.

There is little doubt that Kidd committed a number of outright piracies in the Indian Ocean, but it is equally clear that his trial provided a scapegoat for the establishment figures who had employed him: a full investigation would have exposed both their greed in organizing an anti-piracy mission for their own profit, and their incompetence in choosing a commander so unsuited to the task. Abandoned by his sponsors (who withheld the French pass from the *Quedah Merchant*, which would have been valuable evidence for the defence), Kidd was found guilty of the murder of William Moore and of five counts of piracy. He was sentenced with his shipmate Darby Mullins to be hanged at Execution Dock in May 1701.

Bad luck and humiliation followed him still, turning even his death into a gruesome pantomime. Fortunately the 'Arch-Pirate and common enemy of mankind' was blind drunk when, on the first attempt to hang him, the rope snapped and he fell sprawling into the mud below. The second try was successful. Such was his perceived infamy, however, that the law was not finished with him even in death. His body was tarred and bound in a metal harness, and left to swing from a gibbet at Tilbury Point as a warning to passing seafarers of the perils of piracy. Here it hung for years until time and the elements mercifully consigned it to oblivion.

RIGHT: *Such was the interest in Kidd's case that a full account of his trial was published soon afterwards.*

BELOW: *A nineteenth-century woodcut showing Kidd's body hanging in an iron cage as a warning to any seaman contemplating the pirate life. His body was tarred in order to preserve it as long as possible.*

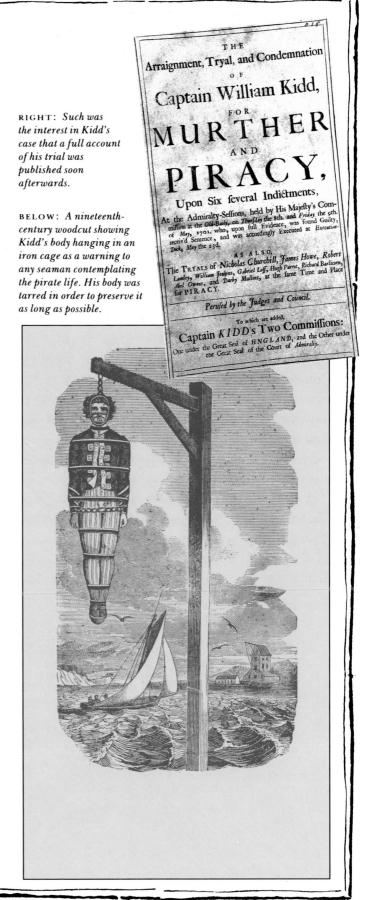

# HENRY AVERY

'Middle-sized, inclinable to be fat, and of a jolly complexion ... His manner of living was imprinted upon his face'. The description seems more appropriate to a self-indulgent businessman than to a notorious sea robber of the great age of piracy. Probably born in Plymouth in about 1653, Avery is known to have been in the English navy in 1690, and served as a midshipman on both the *Kent* and the *Rupert*. The next knowledge we have of him is in 1694 as a member of a privateering expedition, financed by the King of Spain and sent to protect the trade of the Spanish West Indies from buccaneers and French smugglers. And here Avery's piratical career began: at La Coruña on the outward journey he incited a mutiny, seized the *Charles II*, and informer her drunken captain that 'I am captain of this ship now ... I am bound to Madagascar, with the design of making my own fortune, and that of all the brave fellows joined with me'. Renaming his ship the *Fancy*, Avery weighed anchor and set sail for the east and the pirate haven of Madagascar.

His first act of outright piracy was committed against three English ships in the Cape Verde Islands, and a few weeks later he took two Danish ships on the Guinea

ABOVE: *Henry Avery, with the seizing of the Great Moghul's ship* Gang-i-Sawai *taking place in the background.*

coast. By early 1695 he had reached Madagascar and by the end of that year was in command of a fleet of six ships crewed by a cosmopolitan mix of English, Danish, French and Spanish seamen. In September 1695 he committed his greatest crime – one which was to have considerable political reverberations for the East India Company – the seizing of the Moghul's great treasure ship, the *Gang-i-Sawai*.

With the taking of this great prize, which may have yielded as much as £325,000, Avery prudently decided to retire from piracy. Disbanding his fleet, he took the *Fancy* to the Caribbean, where his crew dispersed. A few were captured and later hanged, while legend has it that Avery himself returned to England, carrying a fortune in the form of diamonds. His fate is unknown, although an unsubstantiated account suggests a poetic justice in his end: Avery was swindled of his fortune by West Country merchants who stole his wealth in the knowledge that he could not complain to the authorities. While a credulous public fantasized about his splendid life, Avery, it is said, died in anonymity in a hovel in Bideford in Devon, 'not being worth as much as would buy him a coffin'.

demands for action by the Indian authorities. In England the idea of sending a whole squadron to wipe out the pirates was rejected on grounds of cost, but a private consortium persuaded Captain William Kidd to sail to the Indian Ocean in pursuit of Avery and other notorious pirates. The sponsors of this syndicate, which received royal support in the form of a privateering commission from the King, were motivated by self-interest rather than altruism, and hoped to profit from the booty taken from captured pirates. But far from catching pirates, Kidd soon threw in his lot with them. When in 1698 he seized the *Quedah Merchant*, whose cargo valued at £30,000 was part-owned by a great court noble named Makhlis Khan, the response of the Indian authorities was similar to the aftermath of Avery's seizure of the *Gang-i-Sawai*: as soon as it became known that the pirates were English, the Indian Governor of Surat placed guards on the East India Company's premises, and for a time halted all their trading activities.

In November 1697 the Moghul authorities, increasingly exasperated by the loss of merchant shipping to European pirates, had ordered all the trading companies to take action to suppress piracy. The increasing arrogance of the pirates, and the predominance of Englishmen among them, forced the East India Company to acknowledge a particular responsibility for hunting them down. In 1698 the Surat Council issued instructions for the escorting of native trading vessels, and attempted to win the co-operation of the French and the Dutch in a scheme of coastal patrols. The Dutch were allocated the protection of the sealanes between Surat and the Red Sea, with the French in the Persian Gulf, while the English undertook to control the coastline from Bombay round to Bengal. Not all participating nations were equally enthusiastic, however. When Kidd in 1698 managed to give

the slip to some Dutch and English ships, the English captain blamed his escape on the Dutch who, he suggested, had everything to gain from the embarrassment that the English pirates caused their compatriots who were engaged in legal trade,

... FOR THAT THE DUTCH DO SEEM TO BE VERY GLAD OF THE SCANDAL WE LIE UNDER FOR PIRACY, AND ON ALL OCCASIONS CAST THE ODIUM ON US HOPING IT WILL BE A MEANS AT LAST TO RUIN OUR TRADE.

This use of piracy as a weapon in the struggle for commercial supremacy was also to be used by the Dutch in Far Eastern seas. The Moghul government, however, from time to time reminded the traders of their responsibilities, either by imprisoning and fining them, or by forcing them, as it did in October 1700, to sign bonds promising that they would indemnify Indian trading vessels against losses from European pirates. But as the English gained the upper hand in India in the course of the eighteenth century, they eventually assumed overall responsibility for the suppression of piracy throughout the Indian Ocean.

At the same time as Kidd's departure for the Indian Ocean in 1696, a naval squadron of four ships under the command of Commodore Thomas Warren had set out to destroy pirate nests as far as the Cape. Two years later he commanded a second squadron, this time with instructions to proceed to Madagascar. Although little was actually achieved (and Warren himself died during the commission) it was a signal that the English authorities would no longer turn a blind eye to piracy: trade was becomingly increasingly dislocated, and the Indian authorities looked to the English to contain the menace. A royal proclamation of 1698 declaring a general amnesty to all pirates east of the Cape (with the exception of Avery and Kidd) persuaded a number of pirates to

# DESERT ISLANDS

ABOVE: *Robinson Crusoe's desert island, as seen by a nineteenth-century illustrator of Defoe's novel.*

Desert islands – rather tropical islands, because that is what is implied by the term – have long been associated with piracy. This is partly due to the pirate punishment of marooning. Any pirate found guilty of desertion, or of stealing from his companions, was liable to be marooned on a deserted shore with a bottle of water, a gun and some ammunition. But it is also because islands were a favourite base for pirate operations. The principal bases for the buccaneers in the Caribbean were the islands of Jamaica, Hispaniola and Tortuga, which were strategically well placed for attacks on the Spanish ships voyaging from the New World to Seville. The island of Madagascar was an ideal base for pirates preying on ships homeward bound from India and the Far East. Uncharted islands also provided hiding places from pirate-hunting warships. The mutineers of the *Bounty* selected Pitcairn Island as a refuge because it had been incorrectly charted. Blackbeard's hiding place was an islet off Ocracoke Inlet on the east coast of America.

Works of fiction have reinforced the associa-

*I saw my fate to my great affliction, viz. that I was in an island environed every way with the sea, no land to be seen, except some rocks which lay a great way off, and two small islands less than this, which lay about three leagues to the west.*
**Daniel Defoe, Robinson Crusoe**

tion of pirates and islands. The most popular of R.M. Ballantyne's adventure stories was *Coral Island*, first published in 1850. Washed up on an island in the South Pacific after a shipwreck, three boys live an idyllic existence until one of them is captured by pirates. R.L. Stevenson in *Treasure Island* was responsible for linking buried pirate treasure with islands. Captain Hook and his pirate crew in *Peter Pan* operate from Kidd's Creek which lies on one side of the island of Never-Never Land. The adventures of the children playing pirates in Arthur Ransome's *Swallows and Amazons* take place on Wild Cat Island, and in *Peter Duck*, Ransome describes the voyage of a schooner crewed by the Walker children and the Blackett sisters to an island in the West Indies where they encounter Black Jack the pirate.

But it is Robinson Crusoe's island which must take first place among desert islands. Although Defoe placed his fictitious island off the east coast of South America, he based his story on the true adventures of a Scottish sailor, Alexander Selkirk, who spent four years stranded on the uninhabited island

of Juan Fernandez off the coast of Chile. William Dampier, the buccaneer and explorer, was commander of the ship which dropped Selkirk on the island. Selkirk had demanded to be set on shore following an argument with the leaders of the expedition. He changed his mind as the ships sailed away but it was too late, and he had to survive on his own until an English ship commanded by Captain Woodes Rogers called at the island in 1709.

Unlike the marooned pirates, Selkirk had been left on the island with some useful equipment. According to Woodes Rogers's account, 'He had with him his Clothes and Bedding, with a Fire-lock, some Powder, Bullets, and Tobacco, a Hatchet, a Knife, a Kettle, a Bible, some practical Pieces, and his Mathematical Instruments and Books'.

RIGHT: *The island of Juan Fernandez where Alexander Selkirk, the model for Robinson Crusoe, was marooned between 1705 and 1709. This map comes from William Hack's* Waggoner of the South Sea, *made in 1684.*

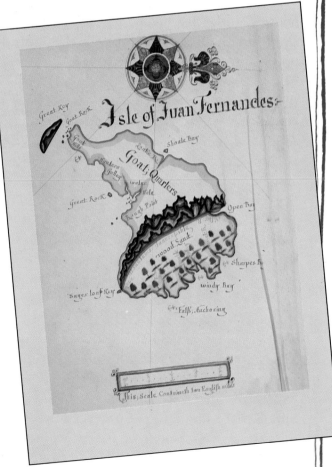

abandon their old way of life, while a new act of Parliament for the more effective suppression of piracy of 1700, and the hanging of many (twenty men were condemned and hanged in one batch in June 1700) were also measures that gradually reinforced the message that the game was no longer worth the candle. By the second decade of the eighteenth century a greater naval presence was having some success in controlling the European pirate menace based at Madagascar, and the numbers of pirates were dwindling. Individual piratical acts continued to occur for the rest of the century and beyond, but with declining frequency and without the previously devastating effects on trade and the commerce in the area.

## WAR AGAINST THE MARATHAS

But no sooner had one threat been demolished than another rose in its place: the Maratha 'pirates' of the west coast of India. The Maratha kingdoms had grown in strength as the Moghul emperor's power waned, and by the early 1700s, in addition to their mountainous homelands in the Western Ghats, they controlled the adjoining seaboard from Bombay to Goa. As sovereigns of the small kingdoms along the west coast, the Marathas naturally considered it their right to control and levy taxes on merchant shipping passing through their waters. They therefore resented the East India Company's assumption that the vessels it licensed should not be bound by such customs regulations. The rise of Kanhoji Angria, a remarkable Maratha leader determined and able to assert his rights over local sea trade, was to disrupt commercial relations in the area for half a century, and inevitably led to the Marathas being classed as pirates alongside all the other pirate fleets operating in the area.

Kanhoji Angria became second-in-command of the Maratha fleet in 1690, and in 1698 he rose to the position of *Surkhail* or Grand Admiral and Viceroy of the Konkan, whose coastline stretches from Bombay south to Mangalore. Angria built up his navy of swift-sailing 'grabs' (from *ghurab*, a kind of square-rigged frigate) as well as erecting a series of heavily fortified castles along the rocky coast south of, and perilously close to, the English base at Bombay. The sinking of East India Company vessels, and in 1712 the kidnapping of the wife of a Company employee travelling to Bombay, brought matters to a head; the crisis was temporarily defused and a treaty signed between Angria and the East India Company in 1713, by the terms of which the Marathas agreed not to molest the Company's ships. This agreement soon foundered on the interpretation of what constituted an English ship and whether, as the Company argued, it included all vessels carrying English cargoes. Soon Angria, whilst always professing a willingness to negotiate, was again asserting his rights to seize ships that had not paid his levy. In 1715 the new Governor of Bombay, Charles Boone, decided on an aggressive forward policy against the Marathas, and began constructing ships in preparation for an all-out assault on the pirate strongholds. While this build-up of forces played an important role in the founding of the Bombay Marine, the forefather of the Indian Navy, there is little doubt that the English abused the spirit if not the letter of their agreement with Angria, granting customs exemption licences to any vessels of any nationality willing to pay. In 1718 another crisis was precipitated with the seizure of one of Angria's ships while it was peaceably employed in Bombay Harbour. The action led to Angria's celebrated threat (not to be taken lightly given the forces at his command) that 'from this day forward, what God gives, I shall take'. In suc-

ceeding years the Marathas stepped up their activities, but first of all the English decided on an all-out assault on the pirate bases.

There followed a series of farcically inept attempts by the authorities in Bombay to capture the string of Angrian fortresses dotted along the coast to the south. A siege of the fort at Gheriah ended in total failure, and even the construction of a 'great and mighty floating machine', *The Prahm*, had little effect. This astonishing contraption was described by Clement Downing as 'a floating castle, or a machine that should be almost cannon-proof. This vessel was pretty flat . . . and [had] but six foot hold; the thickness of her sides was made by the nicest composition cannon-proof.' The intention was that this heavily armoured vessel would be able to approach close enough to the forts to deliver a crippling bombardment to its defences. The seemingly impregnable and unwieldy raft was first tested at Gheriah in 1721, where it performed miserably; later experiments were equally disastrous, and *The Prahm* was finally unceremoniously towed out to sea and burnt. Governor Boone's assaults on Angria had ended in humiliation, and after his departure an uneasy stalemate ensued, punctuated by acts of piracy and reprisal, until Angria's death in 1729.

After a brief period of calm during which the sons of Kanhoji Angria fought amongst themselves for power, hostilities with the East India Company were resumed. The greatest humiliation was the capture of the East Indiaman *Derby* in 1735, which surrendered after a half-hearted struggle and was taken to the Angrian stronghold at Severndroog. Not only did the ship contain the annual shipment of gold for Bombay, but her cargo of ammunition and naval stores supplied the Angrians with vital supplies. Such outrages continued throughout the 1740s under the leadership of Tulaji Angria, son and successor to Kanhoji.

The turning point in English fortunes came in the person of William James of the Bombay Marine. James had been commander of the *Guardian*, built by the East India Company in 1751 specifically to protect the Malabar trade, and in 1755 he decided to confront the Angrians head-on. Leading a small squadron of four ships, he took the 40-gun *Protector* so close to

# THE PIRATE'S CODE
## *of* CONDUCT

ABOVE: *An evocative depiction by
Howard Pyle of a pirate marooned on a
desert island by his shipmates.*

The usual picture of pirates is of bands of lawless desperadoes motivated solely by greed and avarice, rather than men whose lives were governed by strict rules and regulations. Yet one of the earliest authorities on pirate life, Captain Charles Johnson in his book *A general history of the robberies and murders of the most notorious pirates,* first published in 1724, re-prints examples of the codes of conduct which, he maintains, pirates had to sign.

These rules, based on those issued on privateering vessels, set out to regulate the buccaneers' life at sea, ensuring that the disputes which were bound to blow up in the closed world of a pirate ship were settled according to their rules, that booty was equitably shared, and that the pirates were paid compensation for any injuries sustained whilst on 'active service'.

Johnson gave some real-life examples. On board the REVENGE, captained by John Phillips, officers were chosen at the start of the voyage and a form of constitution agreed to 'settle their little commonwealth to prevent disputes and wrangling afterwards'. The articles were then written out and 'all swore to 'em upon a hatchet for want of a Bible':

*i. Every man shall obey civil command: the Captain shall have one full share and a half in all prizes: the master, carpenter, boatswain and gunner shall have one share and a quarter.*

*ii. If any man shall offer to run away or keep any secret from the company, he shall be marooned, with one bottle of Powder, one bottle of water, one small arm, and shot . . .*

*v. That man that shall strike another whilst these articles are in force shall receive Moses' Law (that is 40 stripes lacking one) on the bare back . . .*

*vii. That a man that shall not keep his arms clean, fit for an engagement, or neglect his business, shall be cut off from his share, and suffer such other punishment as the captain and company shall think fit.*

And he sets out some of the rules that the pirates on Captain Bartholomew Roberts's ship were bound to obey:

*i. Every man has a vote in affairs of moment: has equal title to the fresh provisions or strong liquors at any time seized, and [may] use them at pleasure unless a scarcity make it necessary for the good of all to vote a retrenchment.*

*ii. . . . If they defrauded the Company to the value of a dollar, in plate, jewels or money, marooning was the punishment. If robbery was only between one another they contented themselves with slitting the ears and nose of him that was guilty, and set him on shore, not in an inhabited place but*

*somewhere where he was sure to encounter hardships.*

*iii. No person to game at cards or dice for money.*

*iv. The lights and candles to be put out at eight o'clock at night. If any of the crew after that hour still remained inclined to drinking, they were to do it on open deck . . .*

*v. To keep their piece, pistols and cutlass clean and fit for service.*

*vi. No boy or woman to be allowed among them. If any man were found seducing any of the latter sex, and carried her to sea disguised, he was to suffer Death.*

*vii. To desert the ship or their quarters in battle was punished by Death or Marooning.*

*viii. No striking another on board, but every man's quarrels to be ended on shore, at sword and pistol . . .*

*ix. No man to talk of breaking up their way of living till each had a share of £1,000. If, in order to do this, any man should lose a limb or become a cripple in their service, he was to have 800 dollars out of the public stock, and for lesser hurts proportionately . . .*

*xi. The musicians to have rest on the sabbath day, but the other six days and nights none, without special favour.*

All very different from the usual view of piratical anarchy, carousing and sudden violence, these rules – if obeyed – were a living example of 'honour amongst thieves'.

# PIRATES
## *of the*
# BOARDS

Pirates long prowled in the margins of drama before swaggering on to the Romantic stage at the end of the eighteenth century. With their brothers in crime – smugglers, robbers, brigands and bandits – they joined a list of popular 'gothick' villains in melodramas of the early 1800s. The great age of piracy, long gone, had by then acquired a mythical gloss and dramatists seized on any source adaptable to a market hungry for theatrical thrills. Captain Johnson's much reprinted *General history of the pirates* and the nautical novels of the American J. Fennimore Cooper, in parti-cular, proved ready grist to their mill.

The defeat of pirates on stage gave splendid opportunities for ship and fight scenes, with explosions, crashing rigging and glorification of the Navy and 'brave British Tars', a lucrative theme in the age of Nelson.

The first notable pirate spectacle was James Cross's *Blackbeard; or, the Captive Princess* of 1798, 'a serio-comic ballet in two acts': the title neatly yokes archetypal pirate villain with the innocent heroine always threatened in these plays. In 1829 Edward Fitzball, the hack playwright who practically invented nautical melodrama, created a fine pirate in the eponymous villain of *The Red Rover* (from Cooper). Both these pieces became staples of the 'penny plain, tuppence coloured' toy theatre repertoire, to which R.L. Stevenson paid tribute in an essay of 1884, shortly after publishing *Treasure Island*.

Few enthusiasts for Gilbert and Sullivan's *Pirates of Penzance* (1880) now recognize how much Gilbert's script parodies Fitzball and others. Gilbert's soft-hearted pirates turn melodramatic convention on its head by re-fusing to rob orphans – which their victims always claim to be – because they are orphans themselves! All are finally revealed as patrio-tic 'noblemen who have gone wrong'. By the time of this operetta, the melodramas it affectionately guys were long out of fashion, though another echo of their pirates survives in *Peter Pan* (1904). It was Holly-wood and cinema which next recognized the pirates' potential and, at one further remove from both horrid truth and melodramatic caricature, turned them into romantic heroes.

ABOVE: *The programme for the first performance of* The pirates of Penzance *at the Opera Comique in 1880.*

ABOVE: *Commodore Sir William James (1721-1783) by Sir Joshua Reynolds. James commanded the Bombay Marine from 1751-59 and was responsible for the destruction of the Maratha fortresses at Severndroog and Gheriah.*

the fort at Severndroog that few of the defenders' guns could be brought to bear on the vessel, and subjected the castle to a steady bombardment for two days, culminating in the explosion of the magazine and the surrender of the garrison. In February 1756 the remaining fort at Gheriah was taken in a combined operation in which the land forces were led by Robert Clive. The age of Clive and the gathering impetus of British power in Asia had by the end of the eighteenth century largely brought the pirate menace under control. But it was James who had destroyed the Angrian stranglehold on English trade, and he received sufficient government reward to retire to a farm near Eltham in Kent. On nearby Shooter's Hill a folly known as Severndroog Castle, a memorial to James's triumph raised by his widow, stands to this day, a 'monumental tower', which 'records the achievements of the brave, and Angria's subjugated pow'r who plundered on the eastern wave'.

LEFT: *The capture of Gheriah in February 1756, oil painting by Dominic Serres.*

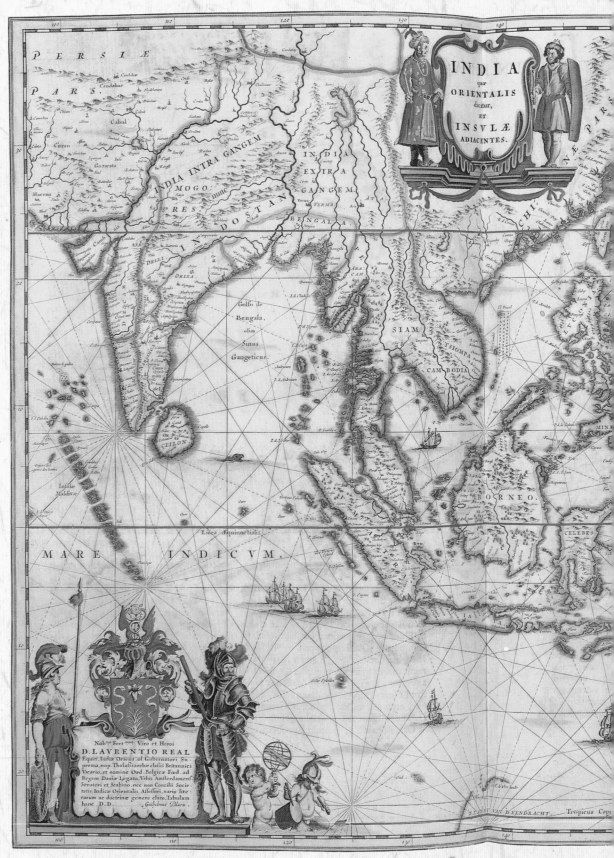

ABOVE: *Map of Southeast Asia and the Far
East, from Joan Blaeu's* Atlas Maior.

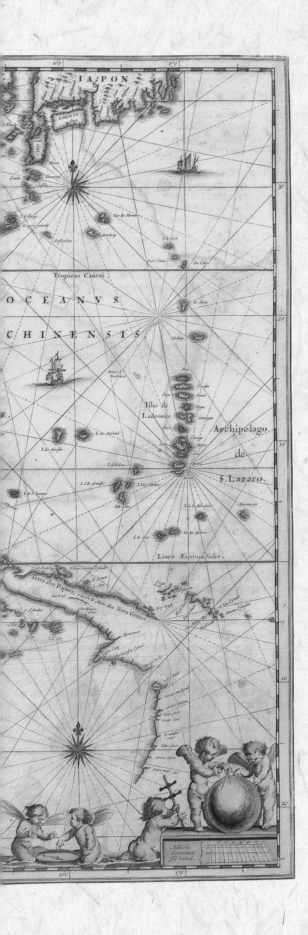

# Great Robbers and Corsairs amongst those Ports of China

## THE EASTERN SEAS

The sixteenth-century navigator Sir Humphrey Gilbert recorded instances of 'the great and dangerous piracy in these [Chinese] seas' that went back to at least AD 400, when the famed San-Wen ravaged the northern seaboard of China and raised a rebellion in the south. In the succeeding centuries both Chinese and Japanese pirates roamed these seas, attacking each other's shipping and coastal settlements. At the height of their power in the early sixteenth century Japanese pirates sailed as far as the Strait of Malacca between Sumatra and Malaysia in search of prey, and such was their ferocity that their ships were barred from every port in Portuguese India. This was warfare as much as piracy, and much of the violence was done by warlords who controlled huge fleets and sometimes armies too. This tradition lived on in the most notorious of the great pirate dynasties that ravaged the coast of China from the seventeenth to the nineteenth centuries – for piracy was one weapon among many in their aspirations to political and even imperial power. A further complicating factor was the arrival of European traders in significant numbers in the sixteenth century.

The Portuguese were the first Europeans to trade in the Far East. In 1516 Alfonso de Albuquerque, Captain General of recently captured Malacca, sent a junk to Canton to trade, and it was not long before more of his countrymen were tempted by the commercial opportunities of the Chinese Empire. In 1518 Simon de Andrada established himself near Macao, built a fort and began a career of systematic robbery, violence and piracy. He was driven from the coast in 1521, but more of his fellow Portuguese arrived to take his place and by the last quarter of the sixteenth century Portugal, from her base at Macao, controlled most of the carrying trade between China and Japan.

The English circumnavigator Thomas Cavendish reached the Far East after having seized the Spanish galleon *Santa Anna* off the coast of California in 1588, and returned to Plymouth 'under a suit of silken sails' which he had probably plundered from the Chinese junk he had taken in the Strait of Sunda – and with the arrival of the English and the Dutch a new chapter of plunder and robbery in the China Seas began. In 1592 James Lancaster, who was later to command the East India Company's first voyage, arrived from the west in the *Edward Bonaventure*. Off Malacca he

seized the Portuguese cargo from a Burma vessel and shortly afterwards attacked another Portuguese ship. Sir Edward Mitchelbourne in the *Tyger*, bound for Patani on the east coast of Malaysia, acted with equal rapacity in 1605, but was nearly undone by greed. Seizing a junk, which unbeknown to him had already been taken by Japanese pirates, his men boarded her and started to rummage for spoil. The Japanese pirates then boarded Mitchelbourne's own ship, snatched weapons and attacked the English. The Japanese were only overcome with the greatest difficulty and fought to the last man. This did not, however, dissuade Mitchelbourne from making further attacks on Chinese junks during his voyage.

That same sense of racial superiority which had characterized dealings in the Indian Ocean surfaced again in the Far East, where in 1608 William Finch, an early East India Company employee, noted that 'some Europeans think it lawful to make prize of the goods and ships of the Ethniks [ie heathens]'. The English were no less culpable than the Portuguese in such matters: in February 1621 John Byrd wrote to the East India Company (which had originally been founded to trade with the Far East rather than India) that the commanders of Company ships had taken three rich China junks, and had sold the booty on their own behalf and not the Company's. It appears that the East India Company had no objection to, and indeed encouraged, its officers to cruise for prizes as well as to trade in the China seas.

## CHING-CHI-LING: FOUNDER OF A PIRATE DYNASTY

The first of the great Chinese pirates whose career is well documented appeared on the scene soon after the ships of the newly formed Dutch and English East India Companies

## *The* PIRATE JUNK

Pirate junks were converted from captured trading vessels by the addition of guns. Larger three-masted vessels were about 80 feet in length, with a beam of about 18 feet, while the smaller two-masted junk was about half the length. The captain lived with his wife (or wives) and children in the poop, while the crew and their families were accommodated in dormitories in the cargo holds or on the open deck. The ship's magazine was in the middle of the crew's quarters in the hold, and an armoury of muskets and pistols was kept under the captain's eye in the poop. The galley was on the after-deck.

sailed into eastern waters in the early 1600s. Ching-Chi-ling, a Roman Catholic convert also known as Gaspar Nicholas, was serving the Dutch East India Company as an interpreter in the 1620s, and appears to have become involved in piracy through an uncle who owned a number of junks. By the end of 1627 his fleet was causing such serious problems that the Dutch Governor of Batavia reported to his masters that the coastal towns and villages of China lived in fear of pirate raids, while 'commercial navigation has totally ceased'.

Ching-Chi-ling terrorized the coast from the Yangzte to Canton with a fleet of 1,000 pirate junks, living in splendour with a bodyguard of Dutch soldiers and a troop of 300 Christian negroes, ex-slaves from Macao whom he dressed in brightly coloured silks. His growing power seems to have kindled even more splendid dreams of influence and authority, and he now 'fed his mind with such lofty dreams that he thought of royalty and the Imperial crown'. Combining piracy with more orthodox enterprises, Ching had accepted a commission in the Chinese Imperial navy, but these were the closing years of the Ming Dynasty, and an offer of an official position and a title from the Tartar invaders of China so appealed to his ambitions that in 1646 he journeyed to Foochow and straight into an ambush. He was imprisoned by the Tartar emperor until his execution in 1661.

Ching-Chi-ling's fleets were taken over by his son Koxinga, who proved a worthy heir. Fuelled by hatred of the Tartar rulers who had tricked, imprisoned and finally killed his father, Koxinga initiated a campaign of revenge: so effective was his piracy that in 1662 the Emperor was forced to order the evacuation of the coast to a depth of twelve miles inland. On his death in 1663 Koxinga was succeeded by his own son, but none of his

ABOVE: *This lithograph, from a watercolour by Edward Cree, shows the destruction of Chui Apoo's pirate fleet in Bias Bay near Hong Kong in September 1849.*

## LIFE WITH THE CHINESE PIRATES

descendants could maintain the empire he had built up, and his fleets split up into smaller groups ruled by individual warlords. For men like Ching-Chi-ling and Koxinga, piracy was just one factor in a larger political picture. In the turbulent years of a dying dynasty, in a country riven by opposing regimes, political uncertainty and official corruption, piracy became so mixed up with rebellion that it is well-nigh impossible to separate it from the political life of the country: which led to piracy being considered a patriotic and honourable activity – whether directed against Europeans or their own people – for generations of Chinese. The piracy continued, but no leader of comparable quality arose to take the place of Ching-Chi-ling for another century.

In the 1760s most piracy was centred around the islands at the mouth of the Canton River, the main outlet for European trade. These islands, among which was the future colony of Hong Kong, were named the Ladrones by the Portuguese, from their word for robber or brigand. Towards the end of the century attacks on European vessels grew more common, and the early years of the nineteenth century saw the rise of another great pirate potentate, Ching Yih, who built up a large fleet which was more than a match for the corrupt and demoralized Imperial navy. By 1805 his control of the coast around Canton was almost complete, and even the appearance of British warships did not intimidate his ships: when in 1807 HMS *Phaeton* and HMS *Bellona* arrived in

China to escort the local ships, the pirates made an expressive display of their contempt:

ABOUT 60 OR 70 SAIL OF LADRONES PASSED IN THE MOST IMPUDENT MANNER WITHIN RANGE OF THE GUNS . . . DETERMINED TO PUNISH THE PRESUMPTION OF THESE PIRATES . . . THE FRIGATE OPENED A SMART FIRE ON THEM WHICH WAS RECEIVED BY THE LADRONES WITH THE UTMOST COOLNESS AND INDIFFERENCE, AND WITHOUT EVEN RETURNING A SHOT.

A European who fell into the hands of Ching Yih in the early 1800s has left a valuable account of his captivity. John Turner, chief mate of the *Tay*, was captured and held for ransom by Ching Yih for five months in 1806–7. He estimated the size of Ching Yih's fleet as between five and six hundred vessels, divided into six squadrons, each one flying a flag of a different colour. Each squadron cruised for prey along its own allotted area of the China coast. The largest of the vessels

carried twelve guns, and these bigger junks also carried rowboats which were capable of carrying twenty men and were armed with swivel guns. These smaller boats were used for boarding other ships or for making surprise attacks on coastal villages. Rules of engagement were similar to those in use by pirates in other oceans: a ship which surrendered without resistance was relieved of its cargo alone. The crews of vessels which put up a fight could expect no such leniency, however, and might be tortured, murdered or held for ransom. The squadrons usually operated individually, but would band together for major expeditons, or if danger threatened. No trading vessel which had not obtained a pass from them was safe, but these passes, once acquired, were respected by all the other pirate squadrons.

Living conditions were spartan in the extreme – especially for a prisoner – and Turner's food consisted of meagre portions of coarse red rice, occasionally enlivened with

BELOW: '*A boatload of piratical rascals*', *sketched by Edward Cree.*

some salt fish. His nights were spent below decks in dark and foetid squalor, crammed into a sleeping space eighteen inches wide and four feet long. He was beaten, kicked and threatened with death regularly, but his sufferings pale into insignificance beside the fate of officers of the Chinese navy who fell into the hands of the pirates. For such unfortunates a swift death was the best they might hope for, and Turner himself witnessed some dreadful scenes of revenge:

> I SAW ONE MAN ... NAILED TO THE DECK THROUGH HIS FEET WITH LARGE NAILS, THEN BEATEN WITH FOUR RATTANS TWISTED TOGETHER, TILL HE VOMITED BLOOD; AND AFTER REMAINING SOME TIME IN THIS STATE, HE WAS TAKEN ASHORE AND CUT TO PIECES. [ANOTHER PRISONER] WAS FIXED UPRIGHT, HIS BOWELS CUT OPEN AND HIS HEART TAKEN OUT, WHICH THEY AFTERWARDS SOAKED IN SPIRITS AND ATE ... THE DEAD BODY I SAW MYSELF.

## CHING SHIH, THE FEMALE PIRATE

Ching Yih died in a typhoon in 1807 and was succeeded by his widow Ching Yih Saou, commonly known as Ching Shih. Alexander Dalrymple mentions in his *Memoir concerning the pirates on the coast of China* (1806) that it was not uncommon for Ladrone junks to have female captains, but Ching Shih was an altogether exceptional leader – as much administrator and businesswoman as pirate chief. She kept scrupulously careful records of her business dealings, and required her men to adhere to a list of rules regulating all aspects of pirate life. This code of conduct makes a fascinating comparison with that imposed by the buccaneers in the Caribbean over a century before. Among the most important rules were:

> NO PIRATE MIGHT GO ASHORE WITHOUT PERMISSION. PUNISHMENT FOR A FIRST OFFENCE WAS PERFORATION OF THE EARS; A

RIGHT: *The capture of John Turner, chief mate of the ship* Tay, *by Ching Yih's pirates in 1806.*

REPETITION ATTRACTED THE DEATH PENALTY.

ALL PLUNDERED GOODS MUST BE REGIS-
TERED BEFORE DISTRIBUTION. THE SHIP
RESPONSIBLE FOR THE TAKING OF A PARTICULAR
PIECE OF BOOTY RECEIVED A FIFTH OF ITS
VALUE, THE REMAINDER BECAME PART OF THE
GENERAL FUND.

ABUSE OF WOMEN WAS FORBIDDEN, AL-
THOUGH WOMEN WERE TAKEN AS SLAVES AND
CONCUBINES. THOSE NOT KEPT FOR RANSOM
WERE SOLD TO THE PIRATES AS WIVES FOR $40
EACH.

COUNTRY PEOPLE WERE TO BE PAID FOR
PROVISIONS AND STORES TAKEN FROM THEM.

From accounts that survive, these rules appear
to have been more honoured in the breach
than in the observance. And just as European
pirates assumed a spurious respectability by
referring to their thefts as 'purchase', so Ching
Shih's plunder was known as 'a transhipping
of goods'!

But Ching Shih finally fell victim to her own
success and ambitions. She increased the size
of her fleet and the scope of her operations so
much that Chinese coastal trade was reduced
to a state of terrified and impotent paralysis,
and concerted action against her became
inevitable. Her second in command was Chang
Paou, a lieutenant of her late husband, and
also her lover, and she sailed in his junk at the
head of the Red Squadron, the chief division
of her fleet and as large as the other five put
together. At the height of her power it was
estimated that she controlled a fleet of 800
large junks, nearly 1,000 smaller boats and a
pirate community of some 70,000–80,000 men
and women. The largest of her war junks were
nearly 600 tons, mounting up to thirty guns
and carrying between three and four
hundred men.

Richard Glasspoole, fourth officer of the
East Indiaman *Marquis of Ely*, was captured by
Ching Shih in September 1809, and remained
a prisoner until he was ransomed in December.
His account of this time records the barbarities
of life on board the pirate junks: an existence
of dirt and overcrowding, bad food and
boredom: rats were encouraged to breed and
were considered a delicacy, and 'we lived three
weeks on caterpillars boiled in rice'.

This existence was punctuated by episodes
of horrific violence: on 1 October the squadron
started the systematic plundering of villages
west of Bocca Tigris. Whole settlements were
put to the torch, and the inhabitants kid-
napped for ransom or massacred. Glasspoole's
own men were forced to participate in the
slaughter – at first under pain of death, but
with the incentive of $20 for every head
brought in. As the pirates returned Glasspoole
saw that many of them carried a pair of heads,
tied together by the pigtails and casually slung
around their necks. A few came back with as
many as six heads. Glasspoole seems to have
played an equivocal role in these proceedings,
remaining on board and manning one of the
big guns. He became something of a favourite
of Ching Shih, who before battle would
sprinkle him with garlic water as a charm
against injury.

Ching Shih's downfall finally came about
through dissension amongst the pirates themselves. Jealous of the intimacy between Ching
Shih and her lieutenant Chang Paou, the
commander of the Black Squadron, Kwo Po
Tai, refused to come to his aid in battle. Chang
Paou survived this betrayal, but the next battle
was between the two pirate commanders
themselves. The squadrons met in a savage
engagement at Lantao near the future colony
of Hong Kong: many of the ships were blown
up with all on board, while others held out
while there was still a single man left to fight.
Chang Paou withdrew, the decks of his ships
running with blood amidst the bodies of the

# PIRATE SHIPS

Pirates in different parts of the world used a variety of vessels ranging from the great war junks of the Chinese pirates to the swift oar-powered galleys of the Barbary corsairs. Pirates operating in the Atlantic usually relied on captured merchant ships. Size was less important than speed because the essence of a pirate attack was hit and run. Vessels of shallow draught, which could hide in shallow creeks and be easily beached for repairs, were also favoured.

The vessel shown here is a two-masted schooner of the type much used by pirates on the North American coast and in the Caribbean. The drawing is based on the lines of the *Helena* of 214 tons as she was fitted out at Deptford in 1778. She was 76 feet in length (on deck) and had 22 guns. The schooner *Hispaniola* in R.L. Stevenson's *Treasure Island* was exactly like this. The crew are heaving up the anchor and are preparing to set sail.

CREW SPACE

MASTER

PURSER'S CABIN

MASTER'S CABIN

BREAD ROOM

CAPTAIN'S CABIN

CAPTAIN'S DAYROOM

CAPTAIN

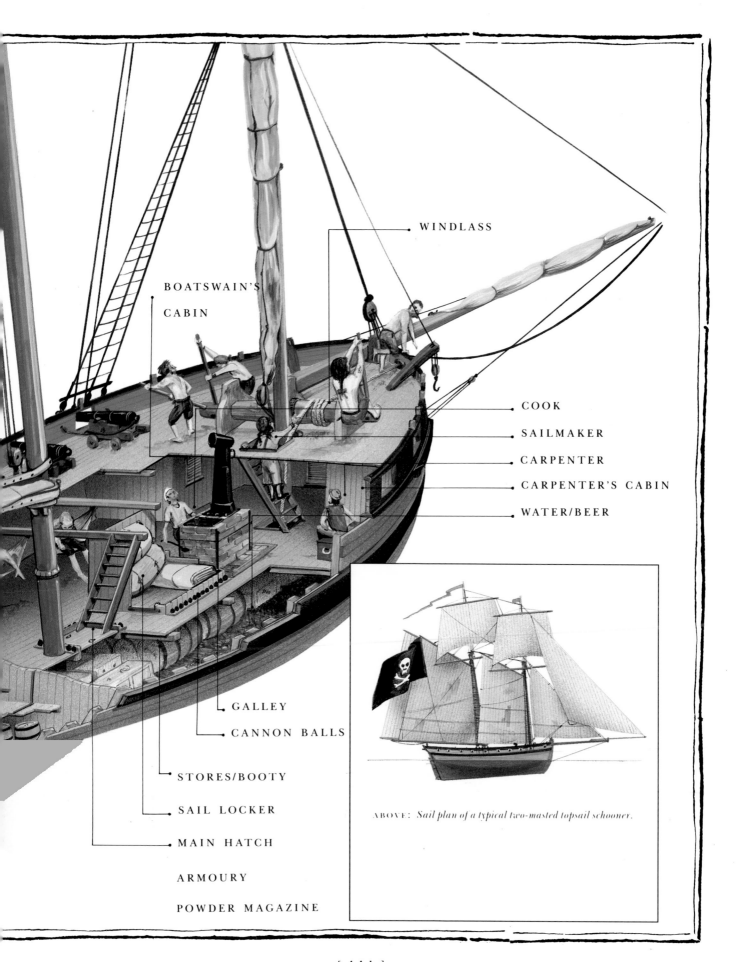

WINDLASS

BOATSWAIN'S
CABIN

COOK

SAILMAKER

CARPENTER

CARPENTER'S CABIN

WATER/BEER

GALLEY

CANNON BALLS

STORES/BOOTY

SAIL LOCKER

MAIN HATCH

ARMOURY

POWDER MAGAZINE

ABOVE: *Sail plan of a typical two-masted topsail schooner.*

dead and dying.

Although he had emerged the victor from this first struggle for power, Kwo Po Tai realized that this breach in the pirate alliance heralded the breaking up of the fleet. He prudently surrendered to the authorities, was created a naval mandarin, and in a *volte-face* that recalls Sir Henry Morgan's enthusiastic suppression of the buccaneers, was employed to subdue the remaining pirates. The news of Kwo Po Tai's desertion and pardon, together with the depletion of her fleet, persuaded Ching Shih and Chang Paou to surrender also. Terms were arranged, and in 1810 her fleet sailed up the river at Canton towards Bocca Tigris with all flags flying. At Canton the fleet was surrendered, and by the terms of the treaty Chang Paou was also appointed to the rank of a naval mandarin, while his men were given the choice of returning to their homes or joining the Imperial navy. Several thousands chose the navy, and under Chang Paou's command cleared the China Seas of their former comrades of the Yellow and Green pirate squadrons. Ching Shih fades from history at this point, although rumour has it that her business acumen was henceforward employed in the smuggling trade – a less hazardous if less renumerative calling.

## THE LAST GREAT PIRATE FLEET

The East India Company's monopoly of the China trade had ended in 1834, and there was a consequent mushrooming of English traders travelling to the east. While the founding of a permanent British settlement in Hong Kong in 1841 ultimately spelled the end of large-scale piracy in the area, in its early years the growing merchant community acted as a magnet for pirates. The greatest of these was Shap-'ng-tsai, who in the course of the 1840s built up a large fleet of pirate junks which terrorized the coast from Fukien south to the island of Hainan in the Gulf of Tonkin. In October 1849 an expedition under the command of Commander Dalrymple Hay was despatched to destroy the pirate fleet. As well as eight junks of the Chinese navy, the East India Company's paddle-steamer *Phlegethon* accompanied the punitive expedition. The pirate fleet was chased for over 1,000 miles before it was cornered in the Tonkin River. The action that followed demonstrated decisively the effectiveness of steam-power against a sailing enemy. Hay's little armada crossed the river bar at the top of the tide and poured a punishing fire into the moored pirate fleet. The first ebb of the tide shifted the pirate junks and, without any means of positioning their ships, their broadside of 240 guns passed completely wide. In the course of the battle and subsequent mopping-up operations 58 junks and 1,800 pirates were destroyed. Shap-'ng-tsai escaped and subsequently received a pardon and a minor appointment from the Chinese authorities, but his pirate days were over. While there were to be further outbreaks of piracy in the following decades, superior technology, allied to a permanent naval presence, had effectively defused the pirate menace on the China Seas.

## 'THE PIRATE WIND': SOUTHEAST ASIA

South of the China coast lies the island chain of Southeast Asia, and this also proved a fruitful hunting ground for pirates. Seafaring bands preyed both on the shipping of the colonial powers and on other tribal groups, taking slaves and merchandise for sale in the markets of the archipelago. Much of this 'piracy' can be seen both as an accepted weapon in the political development of the

# CAPTAIN PUGWASH

Captain Pugwash, who made his first appearance in a comic strip drawn by John Ryan in the *Eagle* in 1950, likes to think of himself as the bravest, most handsome pirate who ever roamed the seven seas. But in fact, this somewhat overweight, incompetent buccaneer — who became a television and video star as well as having more than fifteen books written about him — is something of a coward, who turns to jelly at the approach of his dreaded enemy, Cutthroat Jake. The crew of Pugwash's ship, *The Black Pig*, are a greedy, indolent lot too, all except for Tom, the Cabin Boy, whose pluck and good sense usually save the day.

kingdoms and sultanates of the archipelago, and as an inevitable response to European colonialism. While merchants in Southeast Asia railed against the evil of the pirate menace and its detrimental effect on European trade, it had long been recognized by more far-sighted observers that the word 'pirate', with all its moral implications, was insufficient to describe the complex political and economic situation of the Eastern Archipelago. The development and the composition of small native states with swiftly changing tribal allegiances had no counterpart in European political systems; and the arrival of European merchants and colonialists profoundly altered and ultimately destroyed a fragile and intricate web of inter-island commerce. John Crawfurd neatly summed up the double standards of his compatriots in his *History of the Indian Archipelago* (1820):

ABOVE: *A watercolour by Edward Cree showing pirates being killed by villagers after the destruction of Shap-'ng-Tsai's fleet in October 1849: 'The Cochins were chasing the poor wretches in their sampans and spearing them in the water'.*

# PIRATE LIFE

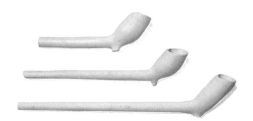

ABOVE: *This onion-shaped bottle, clay pipes and tankard are among the thousands of objects that have been retrieved by archeologists in recent years from the seabed around the famous buccaneer centre of Port Royal, Jamaica.*

When a pirate ship returned to her home base in Jamaica or Hispaniola after a successful raid on the Spanish Main, the crew went ashore and indulged in an orgy of riotous living. Exquemelin gives numerous examples of how the pirates 'wasted in a few days in the taverns and stews all they had gotten, by giving themselves to all manner of debauchery with strumpets and wine'. Men rampaged up and down the streets blind drunk. One pirate gave a prostitute five hundred pieces of eight 'only that he might see her naked'.

Others lost all their money on gambling. After plundering Maracaibo in 1625 L'Ollonais, the French buccaneer, divided the spoils so that each man received one hundred pieces of eight. He and his men returned to Tortuga and 'in three weeks they had scarce any money left them, having spent it all in things of little value or at play of cards and dice'.

Life was very different when the pirates were cruising the coasts looking for victims to plunder. The priorities then were maintaining the ship in good order and finding enough food and water to keep them going. The journal of Basil Ringrose provides a picture of the routine tasks which occupied a large part of the buccaneers' life. Speed was essential for a pirate ship to enable her to make a successful attack and a rapid getaway. At regular intervals the pirates therefore beached their ship on a secluded shore so they could careen her, an operation which involved scraping the weed and barnacles off the bottom, and putting on some form of anti-fouling layer.

Repairs to spars, sails and rigging were equally essential. While some men carried out these tasks, others went in search of fresh water and food. Sometimes they were lucky. At Drake's Island near San Francisco they caught and salted a large number of goats and turtles. On another occasion they had to eat monkeys and snakes. Sometimes they had to survive on bread and water. Several pirates went down with scurvy which was blamed on 'the great hardship and want of provisions we had endured for several months past'.

It is easy to think of pirates as a race apart: bloodthirsty ruffians isolated by their crimes from the rest of the human race. In fact most were ordinary seamen who had been attracted to piracy by the lure of plunder, or had joined a pirate ship because they could not find work elsewhere. In a sample of seven hundred men tried for piracy between 1600 and 1640 no less than 73 per cent described themselves as mariners or sailors. Many had wives and families. Captain Tew had a wife and children in Newport, Rhode Island. Captain Kidd's wife and daughters lived in New York. Some had several wives: John Ward had a wife in

RIGHT: *A typically romantic view of the pirates' life on the open sea is seen in Howard Pyle's depiction of a swaggering private captain on board his ship.*

ABOVE: *Much of the pirates' ill-gotten gains were dissipated in drink and debauchery. This 19th-century illustration shows Bartholomew Robert's men carousing at Old Calabar River in West Africa.*

England and another in Tunis. John Plantain, a pirate who called himself King of Ranter Bay, lived in Madagascar 'with many wives whom he kept in great subjection ... They were dressed in richest silks and some of them had diamond necklaces'. Pirates rarely took their women to sea and it is significant that the famous female pirates Mary Read and Ann Bonny disguised themselves as men throughout their time at sea.

The artefacts recovered from the sunken city of Port Royal, Jamaica, are a further reminder that pirates were not so very different from ordinary seamen. There can be no doubt that Port Royal was a regular base for privateers, buccaneers and pirates and yet the objects recovered from the sea by the archaeologists are mostly of a domestic nature and would have been common in any English town in the 1690s. They range from pewter plates and tankards, silver spoons and stoneware jugs to brass buckles, clay pipes and candlesticks. There are also maritime artefacts such as shipwrights' tools and navigational instruments, and again these are no different from the items which would have been around in any seaport of the period.

CONDUCT OF THE NATURE HERE RELATED BROUGHT THE EUROPEAN CHARACTER INTO THE GREATEST DISCREDIT WITH ALL THE NATIVES OF THE ARCHIPELAGO, AND THE PIRATICAL CHARACTER WHICH WE HAVE ATTEMPTED TO FIX UPON THEM, MIGHT BE MOST TRULY RETALIATED UPON US.

But prior to 1800 this was a gradual process that did not destroy the traditional trading patterns of those islands outside Dutch control. From the seventeenth century the main impact of the Dutch was seen in a slow fragmentation of the formerly powerful Malaysian states of the archipelago: both the Malays and Javanese lost their predominant position as carriers of trade and, in the case of the Malays, many took to piracy. In the course of the nineteenth century, however, the political pattern of the archipelago was completely revolutionized. The Treaty of London of 1824, which effectively divided Southeast Asia between Holland and Britain, recognized the threat to trade and contained a clause outlining joint action to be taken to deal with piracy.

Just as today, the main sea route to the Far East took sailing ships along the narrow seaway of the Strait of Malacca to the South China Sea. This 500-mile journey along the coast of peninsular Malaya signalled the start of the most perilous part of the voyage, and from here ships sailed within range of the countless islands of the Eastern Archipelago, a huge bracelet enclosing the South China Sea and stretching from Sumatra to the Philippines. These seas were the natural home to one or other of the fleets of marauders and pirates whose sleek shallow-draught *prahus*, rowed by teams of captured slaves, could seem to materialize from nowhere and disappear as swiftly among the inaccessible mangrove

ABOVE: *An Ilanun pirate, from the island of Mindinao in the Philippines. From F. Marryat's* Borneo and the Indian Archipelago *(1848).*

swamps and uncharted creeks of densely forested islands.

From Sulu came the Balanini pirates. To western eyes this sultanate, centred on the island of Jolo in the middle of the Sulu Archipelago to the north-east of Borneo, was the stronghold of piracy. For three centuries it had successfully resisted colonial encroachments, but with the increasing European domination of trade, the opportunities for legitimate commerce diminished, and the men of Sulu increasingly turned to piracy and plunder rather than submit to the authority of Catholic Spain. Attempts by the British to establish their influence also came to nothing. In 1814 Stamford Raffles, future founder of

Singapore, sent John Hunt to Jolo to inform the sultan of 'the establishment of the British Empire in the Eastern Seas', and to negotiate the posting of a British agent to the sultanate, only to be met with the rebuff that 'even though we are pirates, the British have no right to interfere'. The men of Sulu were expert sailors, and their swift *corocoros* (sailing vessels with outriggers and high arched stems and sterns) descended on the unprotected islands of the Philippines in search of slaves for the markets of Southeast Asia – just as their European counterparts cruised the shores of east and west Africa for the valuable human cargo for the American markets. Only in 1851 was the sultanate finally crushed by the Spanish empire in the Philippines.

Further east, the island of Mindinao in the Philippines was the home of the much-feared Ilanuns, whose great fleets captured and traded slaves throughout the archipelago. By the nineteenth century these were the most feared marauders in Southeast Asia, but they do not appear to have taken to piracy on any large scale until the eighteenth century. William Dampier, who lived among the Ilanuns for six months in the 1680s, makes no mention of piracy, describing them as a peaceable people, who purchased the goods they needed with gold from their mines. Dampier found the Malays in general to be an honest race; the piracy that did exist he considered to be a direct response to the economic stranglehold imposed on the archipelago by the Dutch.

The Ilanun and Balanini made regular and well-planned voyages throughout the archipelago, their fleets of large galleys varying in size from 40 to 100 tons, with crews of from 40 to 60 men. From Sulu and Mindinao they sailed to north-west Borneo and there divided into squadrons which roamed the eastern seas. One group would circumnavigate Borneo itself and make attacks on New Guinea

## CHUI APOO

Chui Apoo was the lieutenant of the notorious Shap-'ng-tsai (see page 112), and commander of a formidable pirate fleet in his own right. He was based at Bias Bay, a notorious pirate stronghold only fifty miles east of Hong Kong which was to retain its evil reputation as a haunt of sea robbers right up to the 1930s. Here, in September 1849, he was cornered by a force under Commander Dalrymple Hay, and his fleet was destroyed and over 400 of his men killed. Shore parties destroyed the pirate dockyards and vessels on the stocks, while the arsenal of weapons was confiscated. The destruction of Chui Apoo's fleet cleared the way for the final test of strength with his more powerful master, Shap-'ng-tsai.

Although wounded in the battle, Chui Apoo escaped. He was betrayed by his followers two years later. Sentenced to banishment in 1851, he committed suicide in prison.

and the Celebes on the return journey, while a second headed for the Gulf of Siam and the east coast of Malaya. A third squadron sailed through the Strait of Malacca, sometimes penetrating as far north as Burma, while a fourth headed for the north coast of Java and thence westwards to the Bay of Bengal. A last group was left to pillage among the islands of the Philippines. Such was the regularity of these voyages that the months of August, September and October were known to the British authorities in the Straits Settlements as the 'Lanun Season'.

The Bugis traders from Sulawesi posed an additional threat to European trade, both through their legitimate activities and through piracy. Skilfully navigating between the islands of the East Indies from New Guinea to Sumatra, the Bugis had dominated the seaborne trade of the Eastern Archipelago for centuries. Singapore hosted a Bugis community from the early days of the settlement,

and their ships came to trade each year. The fleet of some two hundred vessels arrived every September and October, loaded with the exotic produce of the east: patterned cloth and gold-dust, tortoiseshell and bird of paradise feathers, spices and edible birds' nests. They combined this legitimate trade with piracy and slave-trading, and had no scruples about attacking European vessels from time to time. A Singapore merchant named Dalton who sailed with the Bugis fleet in 1827, and who was captured by them for two years, described them as 'the most mercenary, bloodthirsty inhuman race . . . and most deadly foes to all Europeans'. He considered 'every Bugis *prahu* . . . a pirate' and claimed to have met one pirate chief who boasted that he had killed the captains of twenty-seven European ships. There were certainly many pirates amongst the Bugis, but the vehemence of these opinions was doubtless influenced by the European desire to break the Bugis' profitable monopoly of the island trade.

## THE FOUNDING OF SINGAPORE

Piracy on the open seas was the greatest threat to the young settlement of Singapore, founded by Raffles in 1819, and the eastern seas saw a resurgence of the menace just at the time when it was being successfully, if slowly, eradicated elsewhere. At the northern entrance to the Strait of Malacca travellers ran the gauntlet of the Achin pirates of northern Sumatra, while at the other end, only a little south of Singapore itself, the Riau-Lingga Archipelago was a veritable nest of pirates. Much of the threat to Singapore was controlled from the island itself. Vessels were attacked within sight of the shore, spies in the town supplied the pirates with information about sailings, and many merchants traded in stolen goods. And

ABOVE: *Chinese pirate flag, reputed to have been captured from the pirate admiral Shap-ng-Tsai in October 1849.*

# PIRATE WEAPONS

*of the East*

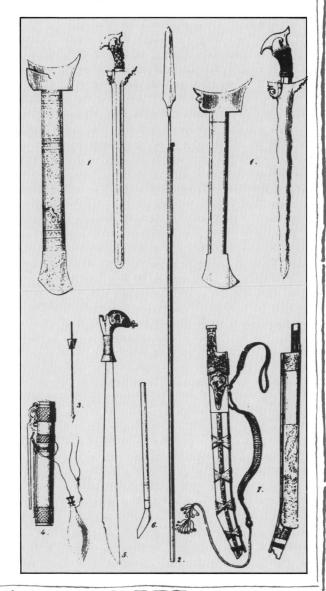

Like the pirates of other oceans, the marauders of the eastern seas were happy to take European guns and swords for their own use when they had the opportunity. Sometimes these were adapted to suit local conditions, like the swivel guns mounted on the prows of the Malay pirate *Prahus*. These followed European prototypes but were of local manufacture. Such brass guns were a prized possession, and would be guarded jealously by the owner and stored in his house when not actually in use during a cruise. But more commonly the pirates of Southeast Asia used indigenous weapons, including spears and *Sumpitans* or blowpipes. This *dao*, decorated with tufts of human hair, was captured during a Royal Navy anti-piracy expedition to the Sulu Archipelago in the 1870s.

The engraving on the right shows a selection of weapons from Borneo, reproduced in Sir Edward Belcher's *Narrative of the Voyage of HMS Samarang* (London, 1848). It shows several *kris* and *parang* (flashing knives or short swords), with a *sumpitan* (blow-pipe) in the centre. The quiver and poisoned arrow for the blow-pipe are seen at the bottom left.

ABOVE: *Admiral Sir Henry Keppel (1808-1904), scourge of the Borneo pirates in the 1840s. His adventures in Southeast Asia are recounted in his* The expedition to Borneo of HMS Dido *(London, 1846).*

for years the European merchant community of Singapore was forced to watch in impotent fury as the Temenggong of Johore, from whom Singapore had been acquired, controlled a pirate network based on the island while simultaneously professing friendship with the English. Singapore was a barely concealed pirate base, and the authorities watched helplessly as heavily armed junks, carrying no cargo, set sail from Singapore with barely concealed piratical intent. Only in the 1840s was the Temenggong Ibrahim persuaded to abandon piracy in favour of legitimate trade.

## THE EAST INDIA COMPANY ACTS AGAINST PIRACY

In 1835 the Resident Councillor Samuel Bonham warned that piracy threatened Singapore and the trade of the archipelago with 'total annihilation', and the merchant community presented a petition demanding that action be taken; in 1836, therefore, the sloop HMS *Wolf* and the East India Company's steamer *Diana* were despatched to clear the Strait of Malacca of pirates. Such was the success of these steamers, whose manoeuvrability was a considerable shock to the pirate *prahus*, that by the end of the year Singapore waters were safe and the vessels extended their operations further afield. But with their departure the situation again deteriorated, and it was realized that the pirates would never be permanently stamped out until their bases throughout the archipelago were destroyed.

The Balanini and Ilanun pirates were based in the Spanish sphere of influence, and it was politically unacceptable to send a British warship to rout them out, but in 1843–4 punitive expeditions along the north Borneo coast had a salutory effect both on Dyak raiders and on the Singapore pirates. The man most responsible for this work was the commander of HMS *Dido*, the diminutive Henry Keppel, who was persuaded by the Rajah of Sarawak, James Brooke, to deal with the Dyaks who preyed on local and foreign shipping from their bases in Borneo. Keppel's intervention in Borneo also strengthened Brooke's political hold over his newly acquired kingdom. In 1843, with additional forces in the form of Dyak levies supplied by Brooke, boats from *Dido* attacked the long-houses of the Saribas, and a second attack in 1844 devastated the Dyak forces. While further outbreaks were to take place in the 1850s, Keppel and Brooke effectively broke Dyak resistance to European rule. Further punitive measures were taken by Sir Edward Belcher who in June 1844 killed 350 alleged pirates in the Moluccas. In 1849 Captain Farquhar of HMS *Albatross* and Rajah Brooke destroyed a Dyak war fleet of 88 boats. Farquhar successfully claimed £20,700 for the Dyaks killed in this action, and the rewards

## RAJAH BROOKE
## *of* SARAWAK

James Brooke (1803–68) captures the romance of an Englishman in the east who became hereditary ruler of a tropical kingdom. Brooke had come to Southeast Asia in his schooner *Royalist* to collect scientific and commercial information which would be of use to future traders. But in Sarawak in 1840 he helped to suppress a local rebellion and was invited to take over the government of the country.

Brooke quickly saw that the main hindrance to the economic expansion of his new kingdom was the disruption to trade caused by piracy. He immediately embarked on a campaign to exterminate this threat. In 1843–4, with the help of naval vessels under the command of Henry Keppel, he mounted a series of daring raids on Dyak pirate strongholds which were often situated far up little-known rivers and could only be reached by small boats. When the story of his war against the pirates reached England he became a national hero, and was knighted in 1848 for his anti-piratical services. Despite a commission of enquiry in the 1850s into his methods of waging war against the Dyak pirates he continued a vigorous campaign of suppression, and the British public continued to be fascinated by the 'White Rajah': by the time of his retirement to England in 1863, the seas around Borneo had been largely cleared of important pirate fleets.

that could be claimed by naval officers (£20 for each pirate captured or killed) certainly played their part in the enthusiasm with which pirates were hunted down and destroyed – sometimes with little firm evidence of criminality.

The destruction of the Ilanun fleet by the Sarawak steamer *Rainbow* in 1862 stamped out one of the greatest pirate threats in the archipelago, and succeeding decades saw piracy in both China and Southeast Asia largely contained by a combination of superior technology and the extension of colonial rule. But piracy has never died away, and the 1980s and 1990s have seen a new upsurge of activity in the seas of Southeast Asia. For while the value of the cargo carried grows, the small crews of the modern ship are less and less able to oppose even small bands of armed robbers who travel in fast launches, and whose bases, like those of their predecessors, are situated in the hidden creeks of little-known islands. Each year sees ships with cargoes worth millions of pounds boarded and ransacked, and in many cases the vessels themselves are stolen and given a new identity. As long as wealth is transported across the largely unpoliced oceans of the world, the pirate will continue to attack this easy prey, carrying on a tradition which goes back thousands of years to the dawn of seaborne trade.

# PIRATES' WHO'S WHO
## (A PIRATE MISCELLANY)

*The following list summarizes the careers of some of the most celebrated pirates, buccaneers and corsairs who flourished between the sixteenth and nineteenth centuries. It is intended to form a quick reference guide to the biographies of men and women who make an appearance in the main body of the text; readers wishing a fuller biographical guide are directed to Philip Gosse's* The Pirates' Who's Who *(London, 1924).*

**KANHOJI ANGRIA** (died 1729)
*Maratha admiral, active 1690s–1710s*
Ruler of Indian pirates based on the coast south of Bombay who waged war on East India Company shipping in the eighteenth century. The Angrians, named after their leader, were tenacious fighters. In 1707 they battled two English frigates, an East India Company ship and two galleots for an entire day before finally capturing the galleots.

**THOMAS ANSTIS** (died *c*.1723)
*Pirate, active c.1718–23*
Member of a formidable company of pirates headed by Bartholomew Roberts and later leader of his own band in the Caribbean. In 1722 Anstis and his crew sent a petition to England in an attempt to gain the King's pardon. On an uninhabited island off the coast of Cuba they whiled away nine months of waiting with such diversions as dancing and a merry mock court where they tried one another for piracy. He returned to piracy but was killed by his rebellious crew.

**HENRY AVERY,** also known as John Every, Long Ben, Captain Bridgman (1665–*c*.1728)
*English pirate, active 1690s*
Known as the 'Arch Pirate', Avery became notorious after attacking the Great Moghul's ship

*Gang-i-Sawai* in the Red Sea in 1696. He took booty worth a fortune in this fierce attack during which passengers were tortured and women jumped overboard rather than face his brutal crew. He became the stuff of legend, the subject of poems, biographies and a play. Avery was never caught and his fate is obscure. It is believed that he died in poverty in Bideford in Devon, after being swindled of his fortune by merchants.

**BARBAROSSA BROTHERS, Aruj** (died 1518) and **Kheir-ed-din** (died 1546)
*Barbary corsairs, active 1500–46*
The brothers Aruj and Kheir-ed-din came to North Africa at the start of the sixteenth century. More than anyone, the Brothers Barbarossa ('Redbeard') were responsible for establishing the power of the Barbary states, and were feared throughout the Mediterranean for their ferocious attacks on Christian shipping and coastal settlements.

**ANNE BONNY**
*Irish-born pirate, active 1720*
Bonny was married to a penniless ne'er-do-well in the Bahamas when she met the swaggering Captain 'Calico Jack' Rackham and joined his pirate ship dressed as a man. When their ship was attacked by a British Navy sloop off the coast of Jamaica in 1720 Bonny and fellow female pirate, Mary Read, drew their pistols and cutlasses and fought like demons. The rest of the pirates, drunk on rum, cowered in the hold. Like Mary Read, she escaped the death sentence at her trial because she was pregnant. Nothing is known of her subsequent fate.

**ROCHE BRASILIANO**
*Dutch buccaneer, active 1670s*

After a long residence in Brazil, Brasiliano came to Jamaica where he joined a pirate ship and was later elected captain. He particularly hated the Spanish and was renowned for his cruelty and enjoyment of senseless violence: 'Many times being in drink, he would run up and down the streets, beating or wounding whom he met, no person daring to oppose him or make any resistance'.

**CHING YIH** (died 1807)
*Chinese pirate, active 1800s*
Commanded a large pirate fleet of over 500 junks divided into five squadrons in the early 1800s.

**CHING YIH SAOU**
*Chinese woman pirate, active 1807–10*
The most celebrated of early-nineteenth-century Chinese pirates. Ching Yih Saou, widow of pirate Ching Yih, commanded a fleet of over 800 junks. Her powerful fleet disintegrated through internal dissention, and she surrendered to the Imperial authorities in 1810.

**CHUI APOO** (died 1851)
*Chinese pirate, active 1840s*
Lieutenant and relation of the pirate Shap-'ng-tsai, he fled from Hong Kong after murdering two Europeans in 1849, and his fleet was destroyed in Bias Bay in September 1849. He was captured and tried in 1851, but committed suicide in prison.

**WILLIAM DAMPIER** (1652–1715)
*British buccaneer, navigator and hydrographer, active 1679–1711*
Dampier briefly joined the buccaneers who crossed the Isthmus of Panama in 1680, and was involved in piracy and privateering during much of his further travels. He subsequently circumnavigated the globe three

times. The most famous, lasting with many adventures from 1683 to 1691, is described in his *A new voyage round the world* (1697). In 1699 he was sent on a voyage of discovery to New Holland (Australia) as commander of HMS *Roebuck*, and in 1708–11 sailed with Woodes Rogers's privateering circumnavigation as navigator.

### SIMON DANZIKER OR DANSER, ALSO KNOWN AS CAPTAIN DEVIL (died 1611)
*Barbary corsair, active 1600s*
Danser was a famous Dutch renegade and was fabulously successful, capturing, burning and sinking vessels in the Mediterranean, and taking 40 ships in only two years. He is reputed to be the captain who introduced the 'round ship' of northern Europe to the corsairs, thus enabling them to break out of the Mediterranean. He was finally hanged in Tunis by his old masters.

### HOWELL DAVIS
*Welsh pirate, active 1719*
Davis was one of the most enterprising and ingenious pirates off the Guinea coast. One of his cleverest exploits was the capture of two French ships in 1719. Davis forced the prisoners of the first ship on deck to masquerade as pirates and hoisted a dirty tarpaulin as a black pirate flag. Bluffed into believing it was a consort, the second ship surrendered.

### SIR FRANCIS DRAKE (*c.*1543–96)
*English admiral, privateer, active 1567–96*
A legendary privateer, Drake was the first captain to take his own ship around the world. During his long career he made no fewer than seven voyages to the Spanish Main in search of treasure, adventure and revenge. One of his most famous exploits was the night attack on Nombre de Dios in 1572. In 1577–80 he made the first circumnavigation of the world by

an Englishman and returned with a cargo of splendid plunder taken from Spanish galleons and raids upon the coasts of Chile and Peru.

### EDWARD ENGLAND (died *c.*1720)
*English pirate, active 1718–20*
England's real name was possibly Jasper Seager. He was for a time an associate of Bartholomew Roberts on the Guinea coast. After a number of successes in the Atlantic and Indian Ocean England was marooned on Mauritius by his crew for his humanity towards prisoners. He made his way to Madagascar in a small boat which he had managed to build and is thought to have died there in poverty.

### ALEXANDRE OLIVIER EXQUEMELIN (*c.*1645–?)
*French buccaneer, active 1660s–90s*
Probably a native of Harfleur in Normandy, Exquemelin was engaged by the French West India Company and went to Tortuga in 1666, where he served for three years. He then he joined the buccaneers, possibly as a barber-surgeon. He appears to have returned to Europe in 1674 but was later in the Caribbean again in 1697 as a surgeon at the attack on Cartagena in 1697. His principal claim to fame, however, is as the author of *Bucaniers of America*, published in Amsterdam in 1678, first English edition 1684.

### JEAN FLEURY OR FLORIN (died 1527)
*French corsair, active 1520s*
In 1523 Fleury seized three ships near the Azores loaded with riches of the Aztec in Mexico bound for the King of Spain. Included in the vast treasure was 'an emerald as large as the palm of a hand'.

### ANTONIO FUËT, ALSO KNOWN AS CAPTAIN MOIDORE
*French pirate, active 1790s*
One of Victor Hugues's captains, the flamboyant Fuët bombarded a Portuguese ship with guns loaded with gold coins after running out of grapeshot and cannon balls.

Legend recounts that Fuët's surgeons worked hurriedly with scalpels to remove coins from the bodies of the dead and dying.

### SIR JOHN HAWKINS (1532–95)
*English admiral, privateer, active 1562–9*
The first English slave trader, Hawkins made three voyages to the West Indies, testing the Spanish monopoly on the Main. His first two ventures brought spectacular returns as he bartered West African slaves for gold, sugar and hides. The final voyage almost met with disaster when Hawkins and his company were surprised by the Spanish in San Jan de Ulua, the port of Vera Cruz, and were lucky to escape after a six-hour battle.

### JAN JANZ OR JANSZ, ALSO KNOWN AS MURAD RAÏS
*Barbary corsair, active 1620s*
The renegade Dutch privateer terrorized Christian shipping in the Mediterranean. In 1627 Janz led one of the most audacious Barbary raids when a fleet of corsairs sailed to Iceland and pillaged the town of Reykjavik, carrying off salted fish, hides and over 400 men, women and children.

### WILLIAM KIDD (*c.*1645–1701)
*Scottish-born privateer and pirate, active 1697–9*
The notorious Captain Kidd was neither particularly ruthless nor successful. A New York merchant who had previously served as a privateer against the French in the West Indies, he was commissioned in 1696 to hunt pirates but after a series of misfortunes began to raid vessels in the Indian Ocean. He was arrested on his return to America in 1699 and sent to England to stand trial for piracy. Kidd bungled his own defence and vital documents were concealed by his former backers. He was hanged at Execution Dock and his body suspended in an iron cage off Tilbury Point for years as a warning to seamen against piracy.

## KOXINGA (1623–63)
*Chinese warlord and pirate, active 1650s–60s*
The son of the pirate Ching-chi-ling, Koxinga waged a campaign against the Manchu authorities to avenge the imprisonment and death of his father. He had numerous successes against the Imperial navy, and in 1661 seized Formosa from the Dutch.

## FRANCIS L'OLLONAIS, ALSO KNOWN AS JEAN-DAVID NAU
*French buccaneer, active c.1660s*
Nicknamed after his birth place at Sables D'Olonne, L'Ollonais was notorious for his cruelty. He sacked Maracaibo in 1666. Accounts of his ferocity during expeditions in New Granada and Nicaragua include a frenzied occasion when he 'drew his cutlass, slashed open the heart of a poor Spaniard, and pulling it out began to gnaw it, saying to the rest, "I will serve you all alike if you don't talk".'

## EDWARD LOW
*English pirate, active 1720s*
Low was a brutal pirate known for his cruel treatment of prisoners. On one occasion he seized a French ship and released all prisoners except the cook who, he said, 'being a greasy fellow would fry well in the fire'. He was strapped to the mast and burnt with the ship.

## SIR HENRY MAINWARING (1587–1653)
*English vice-admiral and corsair, active 1612–17*
Mainwaring was a pirate hunter who became attracted to the colourful and adventurous life of a sea rover. He turned pirate himself and in 1612 sailed to the Mediterranean. He rapidly became a skilled and successful corsair, basing himself on the Atlantic coast of Morocco. He returned to England in 1616, received a royal pardon, and wrote a treatise on the practices and suppression of piracy.

## CAPTAIN MISSON
*French pirate, active c.1690s*
Misson is reputed to have founded, with a renegade priest named Caraccioli, a socialist pirate state called Libertatia (or Libertalia), at Diego Suarez in Madagascar. There appears to be little foundation in fact for this attractive and persistent legend.

## SIR HENRY MORGAN (c.1635–1688)
*Welsh buccaneer, active c.1660s–70s*
Celebrated in ballads as the greatest of the buccaneers, Morgan was leader of the Port Royal buccaneers in the late 1660s. His boldest exploit was the taking of Panama which was thought to be the wealthiest settlement in the New World in 1671. He subsequently became Deputy Governor of Jamaica.

## GRACE O'MALLEY OR GRANIA NI MHAILLE (born c.1530)
*Irish pirate, active c.1560s–80s*
Grace O'Malley was married to two of the greatest chieftains in the West of Ireland. Famed for her passionate love for the sea, she built up a fleet and based her activities on Clare Island in Clew Bay. She renounced piracy in about 1586 and later received a pardon from Elizabeth I.

## JAMES OR JOHN PLANTAIN
*Jamaican-born pirate, active 1720s*
The so-called 'King of Ranter Bay' in Madagascar, Plantain lived in a stockaded fortress and kept many wives, dressing them in silks and jewels and giving them English names such as Moll, Kate, Sue and Peg.

## BARTHOLOMEW PORTUGUES
*Portuguese-born buccaneer, active 1660s–70s*
Renowned for his 'innumerable excessive insolences upon these [Caribbean] coasts, ...infinite murders and robberies'. Bartholomew Portugues escaped from capture several times, but his luck finally turned when his ship was sunk in a storm off Jamaica, and Bartholomew fades from history.

## JOHN RACKHAM OR RACKAM, ALSO KNOWN AS CALICO JACK (died 1720)
*English pirate, active 1718–20*
Known as Calico Jack for his costumes of colourful cotton, Rackham plundered vessels in the Caribbean until tried for piracy and hanged at Port Royal. His pirate wife, Anne Bonny, who was reprieved because she was pregnant told him she was 'sorry to see him there, but if he had fought like a man, he need not have been hanged like a dog'.

## MARY READ (died c.1720)
*English pirate, active 1710s*
Dressed in men's clothes, Read had fought as a soldier in Flanders. Still dressed as a man, she sailed with Anne Bonny as a pirate in the ship of John 'Calico Jack' Rackham. At her trial in 1720 she escaped the death sentence by virtue of her pregnancy, but died of an illness shortly afterwards.

## BASIL RINGROSE (1653?–86)
*British buccaneer, surgeon, active 1679–86*
Ringrose's account of his experiences with Bartholomew Sharp's expedition across the Isthmus of Panama of 1680–2 forms an invaluable account of the day-to-day activities of the buccaneers, and is published in full in Exquemelin's *Bucaniers of America*. He was killed in an attack on Santiago in Mexico on a subsequent buccaneering expedition.

## BARTHOLOMEW ROBERTS (1682–1722)
*English pirate, active 1720–2*
Reputed to have captured as many as 400 vessels off the coast of Guinea and in the Caribbean, Roberts is probably the most successful pirate who ever sailed. A tall, swarthy, handsome man who dressed in fancy clothes and drank only tea, Roberts's four-year career was a dazzling success until he was

shot in the throat during battle with an English man-of-war.

**WOODES ROGERS** (died 1732)
*English privateer, active 1700s*
Rogers led a celebrated privateering expedition which circumnavigated the globe in 1708–11. William Dampier served as navigator on this immensely profitable voyage, which brought back silks, bullion and precious stones plundered from Spanish vessels. An account of the voyage, during which Alexander Selkirk was rescued from Juan Fernandez, is given in his *A cruising voyage round the world* (1712). He later became Governor of the Bahamas and arrived at New Providence in 1718 with a commission to stamp out piracy.

**SHAP-'NG-TSAI**
*Chinese pirate, active 1840s*
Shap-'ng-tsai controlled a large pirate fleet in the 1840s, which was finally cornered and destroyed by a British squadron in the Gulf of Tonkin in October 1849. Shap himself escaped and struck a deal with the Chinese authorities, receiving a pardon and living to a ripe old age.

**BARTHOLOMEW SHARP** (*c.*1650–90?)
*English buccaneer, active 1660s–90*
Sharp was possibly amongst those who plundered Segovia in 1675, and was commander of a barque on the attack on Porto Bello in 1679. In 1680–2 he led a remarkable buccaneering expedition plundering Spanish settlements along the west coast of South America, before returning to the West Indies via Cape Horn. The valuable charts he seized from the Spanish were instrumental in

securing his release from piracy charges on his return to England in 1682. He was later active again in the Caribbean as both pirate and pirate hunter, and is last heard of in the Virgin Islands in 1699. His account of the 1680–2 expedition is included in Exquemelin's *Bucaniers of America*.

**EDWARD TEACH OR THATCH, ALSO KNOWN AS BLACKBEARD** (died 1718)
*English pirate, active 1716–18*
Teach was famed for his alarming appearance and long black beard which he wore twisted in tails with ribbons and and curled back over his ears. To instil fear in his enemies he went into battle with smoking fuses in his hair. No ship resisted Blackbeard who enhanced his reputation for wickedness by exploits such as shooting without provocation a crew member drinking in his cabin. When asked why he stated 'that if he did not now and then kill one of them, they would forget who he was'.

**THOMAS TEW** (died 1695)
*Rhode Island-born pirate, active 1690s*
Tew was described in William Kidd's commission from William III as being 'wicked and ill-disposed'. He returned to Rhode Island in 1694 after a piratical cruise in the *Amity* with a fortune of £100,000. On a second cruise in the Indian Ocean, he joined up with John Avery and was probably killed in the attack on the *Fateh Muhammad* in Septempter 1695.

**SIR THOMAS VERNEY** (1584–1615)
*Barbary corsair, active 1608–9*
Verney, of a distinguished Buckinghamshire family, left England after a dispute over his inheritance and turned corsair.

However, success eluded him. After taking a number of English ships in the Mediterranean, he was imprisoned as a slave on a Sicilian galley, joined the Sicilian army, and died 'in the extremist calamity of extreme miseries' in a hospital in Messina.

**LIONEL WAFER** (*c.*1660–1705)
*English buccaneer, surgeon, active 1680s*
Wafer joined the buccaneers led by Bartholomew Sharp who crossed the Isthmus of Darien in 1679. Returning back across the isthmus with William Dampier, Wafer was accidentally injured and was cared for by the Cuna Indians. His *New voyage and description of the Isthmus of Panama* (1699) is an important early account of the natural history and inhabitants of Central America.

**JOHN WARD** (*c.*1553–1622)
*Barbary corsair, active 1600s–10s*
A commander in the English navy in the early 1600s, Ward incited his men to mutiny and took a ship to the Mediterranean, where he allied himself to the Dey of Tunis and became a successful and wealthy corsair. He took the Muslim name Yusuf Rais, and died of the plague in Tunis.

**JOHN WATLING** (died 1681)
*English buccaneer, active 1670s–81*
'An old privateer and a stout seaman', Watling served with the buccaneering expedition to Panama in 1680, and was elected leader in the place of Bartholomew Sharp in January 1681. He survived in this post only for a few weeks, being killed in an ill-planned attack on the town of Arica on 30 January.

# INDEX

Page numbers in *italic* refer to the illustrations

# SUGGESTED FURTHER READING

The following is a brief guide to a selection of books which will give the general reader a good introduction to the subject. For those wishing to pursue the subject in more depth, a detailed listing of the available published material can be found in volume four of the catalogue of the Library of the National Maritime Museum, Greenwich, *Piracy and privateering* (London 1972).

## GENERAL

Captain Charles Johnson's *A general history of the robberies and murders of the most notorious pirates, and also their policies, discipline and government* . . . (London, 1724) remains a fascinating account of the careers of the most celebrated figures of the great age of piracy, although some of its information must be treated with caution. Two lively general surveys, readable and accurate, are David Mitchell's *Pirates* (London, 1976) and Edward Lucie-Smith's *Outcasts of the sea* (London, 1978). Douglas Botting's *The Pirates* (Amsterdam, 1978) is enhanced by the extensive range of illustrations. Clive Senior's *A nation of pirates: English piracy in its heyday* (Newton Abbot, 1976), is a scholarly and well-written account of English piracy in the period 1600–40, and Roger Villar brings the story up to date in *Piracy today* (London, 1985), a review of piracy throughout the world in recent times.

## THE CARIBBEAN

Alexandre Olivier Exquemelin's classic work, *Bucaniers of America* remains the major contemporary source for the activities of the buccaneers, written by one of their number. Clinton V. Black's *Pirates of the West Indies* (Cambridge, 1989) is a succinct and readable account by the distinguished Jamaican historian. Peter Earle's *The sack of Panama* (London, 1981) is the best of the many biographies of Henry Morgan, and provides a useful corrective to the biased account given by Exquemelin. David Buisseret and Michael Pawson in *Port Royal, Jamaica* (Oxford, 1975) give the most detailed and well-documented history of the buccaneer city and British naval base. For the early period, Neville Williams's *The sea dogs: privateers, plunder and piracy in the Elizabethan age* (London, 1975) is a well-illustrated and authoritative survey, with good biographies of Drake, Hawkins and Gilbert. Robert E. Lee looks at the most famous pirate in *Blackbeard the pirate: a reappraisal of his life and times* (Winston-Salem, North Carolina, 1974), and is particularly interesting on the trials of pirates.

## THE MEDITERRANEAN

Peter Earle's *Corsairs of Malta and Barbary* (London, 1970) is a detailed account of the Mediterranean corsairs, important for drawing attention to the Christian corsairs. Stephen Clissold in *The Barbary slaves* (London, 1977) concentrates on the human side of the story, describing the way of life in the slave communities of North Africa. The European adventurers who threw in their lot with the Barbary states are the subjects of Christopher Lloyd's *English corsairs on the Barbary coast* (London, 1981), while Sir Godfrey Fisher's *Barbary legend; war, trade and piracy in North Africa 1415–1830* (London, 1957) looks at the corsair phenomenon in the broader context of European history and the struggle for power in the Mediterranean.

## THE INDIAN OCEAN

Captain A.G. Course's *Pirates of the eastern seas* (London, 1966) is a broad introduction to the story of piracy from the Gulf of Aden to Japan. The same geographical area is covered in more detail in S. Charles Hill's *Notes on piracy in eastern waters* (Bombay, 1923–8), a treasure trove of information marred only by the lack of an index. John Biddulph's *The pirates of Malabar* (London, 1907) covers the western seaboard of India and the East India Company's struggles with the Marathas.

## THE FAR EAST

The story of piracy on the China coast and in the Southeast Asian archipelago is told in Harry Miller's *Pirates of the Far East* (London, 1970), while Nicholas Tarling in *Piracy and politics in the Malay world* (first published 1963, reprinted Nendeln, 1978) looks at piracy in Southeast Asia in its relation to European colonial incursions into the area. A narrative history of the same area can be found in Owen Rutter's classic *The pirate wind* (first published 1930, reprinted Singapore, 1986). Of the numerous personal accounts of naval officers involved in anti-piracy activities in the Far East in the nineteenth century, the best is Henry Keppel's *The expedition to Borneo of HMS Dido* (first published 1846, reprinted Singapore, 1991). Grace Fox, in *British admirals and Chinese pirates 1832–1869* (London, 1940) details the attempts of the Royal Navy to smash the pirate menace in nineteenth-century China.